De GUSTIBUS PRESENTS
THE GREAT COOKS' COOKBOOKS

Rustic Italian Cooking

DE GUSTIBUS PRESENTS
THE GREAT COOKS' COOKBOOKS

Rustic Italian Cooking

ARLENE FELTMAN-SAILHAC

PHOTOGRAPHS BY TOM ECKERLE
DESIGN BY MARTIN LUBIN

BLACK DOG & LEVENTHAL
NEW YORK

Published by

Black Dog & Leventhal Publishers, Inc.
151 West 19th Street
New York, NY 10011

Distributed by

Workman Publishing Company
708 Broadway
New York, NY 10003

Manufactured in Hong Kong

ISBN: 1-884822-16-9

h g f e d c b a

Thanks to Lidia Bastianich for permission to publish her recipes. Potato Gnocchi with Fresh Sage Sauce appears in *La Cucina di Lidia* by Lidia Bastianich and Jay Jacobs. Copyright © 1990 by Lidia Bastianich and Jay Jacobs. Published by Bantam Doubleday Dell Publishing Group, Inc., New York.

Tirami-sù by Biba Caggiano to be published in *Love Cookbook* used by permission of Slack Publishing.

Lorenza De'Medici owns the rights to her recipes and grants permission to use Noodle Tart; Squab with Juniper Berries; and Cream with Amaretti.

Clams "Al Forno"; Shells "Al Forno" with Mushrooms and Radicchio; and Cranberry-Walnut Tart from *Cucina Simpatica* by Johanne Killeen and George Germon. Copyright © 1991 by Johanne Killeen and George Germon. Reprinted by permission of HarperCollins Publishers, Inc., New York.

Penne with Asparagus; Trout Cooked in Vernaccia di Oristano; and Walnut Tart adapted from *The Food of Southern Italy* by Carlo Middione. Copyright © 1987 by Carlo Middione. Used by permission of William Morrow & Company, Inc., New York.

Marta Pulini's Gelato di Parmigiano to be published in *The Taste of Memory*. Used with permission of Sterling Publishing Co., Inc., 387 Park Avenue South, New York, N.Y., 10016 from *The Art of Italian Regional Cooking* by Francesco Antonucci, Marta Pulini, and Gianni Salvaterra. Copyright © 1993 by Edizioni Il Fenicottero, English Edition Text © 1995.

DEDICATION

I dedicate this book to my family, who loves to eat:

My parents, Adelaide and Stanley Kessler;

My sister, brother-in-law, and niece, Gayle, Stanley, and Amy Miller;

My Grandma Berdie, who opened my eyes to food;

And to Alain Sailhac and Todd Feltman, the two "men in my life who are my favorite dining partners."

ACKNOWLEDGMENTS

During the 14-year existence of De Gustibus at Macy's, many people have given their support and encouragement.

First, my profound thanks to all the wonderful chefs and cooks who have taught at De Gustibus. Special thanks to Francesco Antonucci, Lidia Bastianich, Giuliano Bugialli, Biba Caggiano, Lorenza De'Medici, Roberto Donna, Johanne Killeen and George Germon, Carlo Middione, Marta Pulini, and Claudio Scadutto.

Thanks to my priceless assistants who are always there for me in a million ways: Jane Asche, Barbara Bjorn, Pam Carey, Corinne Gherardi, Yonina Jacobs, Nancy Robbins, and Betti Zucker.

Thanks to Barbara Teplitz for all her help and support throughout the years, and to Gertrud Yampierre for holding the office together.

Thanks to Ruth Schwartz for believing in the concept of De Gustibus and helping to orchestrate its initiation at Macy's.

Thanks to everyone at Macy's Herald Square who has supported De Gustibus at Macy's since its inception, with special notice to the Public Relations and Advertising Departments, who helped spread the word.

Thanks to J.P. Leventhal and Pamela Horn of Black Dog & Leventhal Publishers for providing the vehicle to put our cooking classes into book form, and for being so encouraging.

A special thanks to Jane Asche for her help in the beginning stages of the book.

Thanks to Tom Eckerle for his magical photographs; Ceci Gallini for her impeccable taste and prop design; and

Roscoe Betsill, whose food styling really took this project to another level.

Thanks for photography props to Joe Denofrio at Macy's N.Y.C.; and to Renée and Luca Mattioli in Montemerano, Italy.

Thanks to Marty Lubin for his wonderful design.

Thanks to Mary Goodbody, recipe-testers Deborah Callan and Elizabeth Wheeler, and editors Sarah Bush and Judith Sutton for making the book "user friendly."

Thanks to my agent Judith Weber for her help and advice.

Special thanks to Judith Choate, who shaped all my words into meaningful prose and never ceased to amaze me with her knowledge of food and her patience and calm, and to Steve Pool for getting these words into the computer with smiles and enthusiasm.

Heartfelt thanks to the entire Kobrand Corporation, purveyors of fine wine, especially Cathleen Burke and Kimberly Charles, for opening the door for the marriage of fine wine and great food for the last 10 years.

Finally, thanks to all the faithful De Gustibus customers who have made all our classes spring to life.

Contents

Foreword

Fourteen years ago, the popularity of cooking classes was growing all over the United States. While interest was high, New Yorkers could not always fit an ongoing series of classes into their busy schedules. Demonstration classes seemed to me to be the answer and De Gustibus was born. What began as four chefs and an electric frying pan on a stage developed into more than 350 chefs and cooking teachers demonstrating their specialties in a professionally equipped kitchen for groups of fervent food-lovers.

When we started De Gustibus in 1980, we had no inkling of the variety of cuisines that would become an integral part of American cooking. Since then we have discovered New World Cuisine, Floridian Cuisine, Light Cooking, Fusion Cooking, Cajun Cooking, Southwestern Cooking —you name it! As American and international cuisines have changed and our tastes broadened, De Gustibus has stayed on the cutting edge of the culinary experience. We have invited teachers, cooks, and chefs to De Gustibus both because of their level of recognition in the food world, and because of their challenging, unique, current, and, above all, noteworthy cooking styles.

The goal of the cooking demonstrations at De Gustibus is to make the art of the grand master chefs and cooks accessible and practical for the home kitchen. Each chef leads the way and holds out a helping hand to the home cook.

The results depend as much on the cook's wit, self-confidence, and interest as they do on a great recipe. Thus, students, and now readers of this book, can learn to master the recipes of the most sophisticated chefs and cooks.

The reason De Gustibus demonstration classes are so popular is that they allow the novice the opportunity to feel the passion—as well as to see each professional chef's or cook's technique, order, and discipline. By seeing how each chef's personality influences the final product, serious home cooks gain the confidence to trust their own tastes and instincts. New and unfamiliar ingredients, untried techniques, and even a little dazzle all find a place in the amateur's kitchen.

This book introduces some of the best and most popular menus demonstrated throughout the years. Each dish is designed to serve six people, unless otherwise noted. All the menus were prepared in class and I have done little to alter them, other than to test and streamline recipes for the home kitchen. I have also provided each chef's strategy and Kobrand Distributors' wine suggestions with every recipe.

ARLENE FELTMAN-SAILHAC
1995

8

Introduction

Italian cooking and Italian chefs rank very high at De Gustibus. Their popularity is evident in the enthusiastic enrollment as well as in the anticipatory chatter at the classroom door. As the crowd of students gathers, you can actually feel the joy in the air. It's party time, and the charm of the chefs, the sensual ingredients, and the full-bodied wines all light the spark.

De Gustibus students seem particularly comfortable with their abilities to prepare Italian food at home. Italian cooking does not seem to carry with it the fear that some other cuisines inspire in home cooks. Perhaps it's the perfectly simple ingredients, or perhaps it's our familiarity with so many supermarket and fast-food Italian-influenced "ready-to-eat" dishes that has made Italian cooking seem so accessible.

The chefs who have taught at De Gustibus have crossed all the boundaries of Italian cooking, from the "toe of the boot" to the soaring Alps, and from the sunny Mediterranean to the equally sun-drenched Adriatic. We have learned the history of many different regions because a particular one was the birthplace of one chef, or another chef feels a special affinity for the locale. Our knowledge of Italian ingredients has grown by leaps, while our understanding of the philosophy of great Italian cooking has expanded enormously.

We have learned when to use fresh pasta and when to use dried. We have explored characteristics of different olive oils, and we have developed an understanding of the complexities of the rich red wines and full-bodied whites. We know the difference between imported and domestic prosciutto, Parmesan, and canned tomatoes. We have had the chance to savor the deeply aromatic aged balsamic vinegar from Modena and to sample the varieties of short-grained rices used for risotto. We have enjoyed wonderful meals from the Italian kitchen—from the home, from the trattoria, from the countryside, and from the bastions of stylish urban dining. Each unique, but all delicious!

The first Italian cook to teach at De Gustibus was the ultimate professional, Giuliano Bugialli. We were so excited by his knowledge of the history of Italian food, by his passion for his homeland, and by his ability to share his gifts with our students, that he went on to become the only chef to have taught at every semester of classes since the inception of De Gustibus. And always to a sellout crowd!

De Gustibus students have had the chance to experience both the traditional and the experimental from the Italian table. Whether from the provinces or from the United States, our Italian chefs have brought the best of Italian cooking to our kitchen. As we share these dishes with you, we hope that you enjoy them as much as we have.

STRATEGIES FOR COOKING FROM OUR GREAT CHEFS AND COOKS

Before beginning to prepare any meal, regardless of how simple or how complicated, take the following steps to heart:

1 Read through the entire menu and its recipes in advance.

2 Complete as many recipes or steps as possible ahead of time, taking care to allow time for defrosting, reheating, bringing to room temperature, or whatever the recipe calls for, before serving.

For each menu we have provided a feature entitled "What You Can Prepare Ahead of Time." This provides time-saving hints, for the cook who is preparing the entire menu, or elements of it, and wants to do as much of the preparation before the actual day of the meal as possible. While you may know that many foods taste better fresh rather than reheated, we have included this list for your convenience, to offer suggestions, not required do-ahead instructions.

3 Place all the ingredients for a particular recipe on, or in, individual trays, plates, or bowls, according to the specific steps in the recipe. Each item should be washed, chopped, measured, separated—or whatever is called for. This organizational technique, known as the *mise en place* (from the French, it literally means "putting into place"), is the most

Mise en place tray

valuable lesson we at De Gustibus have learned from the pros. We strongly urge you to cook this way.

Note that when a recipe calls for a particular ingredient to be cut in a certain size or shape, it matters. The final result is often dependent upon the textures and color, as well as the flavor of the ingredients.

4 Use only the best ingredients available. All good chefs and cooks stress this. Try to find the exact ingredient called for, but if you cannot, substitute as suggested in the recipe or glossary, or use your common sense.

5 Rely on your taste buds. They will not lie!

6 Don't forget to clean up as you work.

Use the menu suggestions in full, or plan meals around one or two of the elements from a menu. Immerse yourself in the authenticity and energy of this rustic Italian cooking. You are bound to create some impressive and delicious dishes.

The Cooks

FRANCESCO ANTONUCCI
Chef/Owner, *Remi*, New York,
New York; Santa Monica, California;
Mexico City, Mexico; and Tel Aviv,
Israel

ROBERTO DONNA
Chef/Owner, *Galileo* and *I Matti*,
Washington, D.C.

LIDIA BASTIANICH
Chef/Owner, *Felidia* and *Becco*,
New York, New York

**JOHANNE KILLEEN AND
GEORGE GERMON**
Chefs/Owners, *Al Forno*, Providence,
Rhode Island

GIULIANO BUGIALLI
Noted cookbook author, New York,
New York

CARLO MIDDIONE
Chef/Owner, *Vivande*, San Francisco,
California

BIBA CAGGIANO
Chef/Owner, *Biba,* Sacramento,
California

MARTA PULINI
Executive Chef, *mad.61*, New York,
New York

LORENZA DE'MEDICI
Noted cookbook author, Italy

CLAUDIO SCADUTTO
Executive Chef, *Trattoria dell'Arte*,
New York, New York

Techniques

COOKING PASTA

Pasta, whether fresh or dried, should be cooked in ample boiling, salted water just until it is *al dente*, or still firm to the bite. Usually 2 gallons of water is enough to cook 1 pound of pasta.

To ensure the best possible taste and texture, the chefs always add salt just at the point when the water comes to a boil before adding pasta.

GRATING CHEESE

Italian hard cheeses, such as Parmigiano-Reggiano, should be purchased in chunks and grated as needed. You can purchase a grater made especially for Parmesan cheese in Italian markets or kitchen equipment shops. Alternatively, you can use the traditional 4-sided kitchen grater or even a small Mouli grater. Do not use a food processor—the speed of the blade creates heat, which will change the taste and texture of the cheese.

MAKING BREAD CRUMBS

One slice of fresh bread yields approximately ½ cup fresh bread crumbs.

One slice dried (or toasted) bread yields approximately ⅓ cup dried bread crumbs.

Trim crusts from slices of firm, good-quality fresh or dried white bread. Cut the bread into cubes and place in a food processor fitted with the metal blade. Pulse until crumbs are formed.

Store fresh bread crumbs in a tightly covered container in the refrigerator for up to 3 days.

Store dried bread crumbs in a tightly covered container at room temperature for up to 1 month.

CUTTING VEGETABLES

Into julienne: Using a small, very sharp knife, a mandoline, or an inexpensive vegetable slicer, cut vegetables into thin, uniform sticks, usually about ¼-inch thick and 1 to 2 inches long. This process is easiest when each vegetable is first cut into uniform pieces. For instance, trim a bell pepper into two or three evenly shaped pieces and then proceed to cut into julienne.

Into dice: Trim vegetables into uniform rectangles. Using a very sharp knife, cut into strips ranging in width from ⅛ to ¼ inch, depending upon the size dice you require. Lay the strips together and cut into an even dice by cross cutting into squares ⅛ to ¼ inch across. When dicing bell peppers, it is particularly important to trim all the membranes and ridges so that you have an absolutely smooth rectangle.

TOASTING AND SKINNING NUTS

Preheat oven to 400 degrees F. Lay the nuts in a single layer on a baking sheet or pie tin. Using a spray bottle such as those used to mist plants, lightly spray the nuts with cool water. Roast for 5 to 10 minutes, depending on the nut's size and oil content, or until golden. Remember, since nuts have a high oil content, they can burn very quickly. Immediately remove from oven and transfer to a cool plate or tray to cool. If you leave them on the baking sheet, they will continue to cook. If the nuts have skins, immediately spread them on a clean kitchen towel. Let them cool slightly and then wrap them in the towel and rub the nuts back and forth to remove the skins.

If you do not need to toast nuts but want to skin them, put them in boiling water for 1 minute. Drain well. Place in a clean kitchen towel and rub the nuts back and forth to remove skins.

MAKING CHOCOLATE CURLS

For ease of handling, you will need at least a 4-ounce solid block of cool, room-temperature chocolate. Using a paper towel, grasp one end of the chocolate block, holding it so that the paper protects it from the heat of your hand.

Using a very sharp potato peeler, gradually peel off a thin sheet of chocolate from the top to the bottom, moving the peeler toward you. The chocolate will curl as it peels off the block. The lighter the pressure, the tighter the curls will be. If the chocolate is too warm, it will not curl; if it is too cold, it will break into slivers.

GRATING CHOCOLATE

Small amounts of solid, room temperature chocolate may be grated on a nutmeg grater. Larger amounts can be processed in a food processor fitted with the metal blade. Grate only as much as you need, since if stored, grated chocolate tends to melt back together.

Pantry Recipes

We supply standard stock recipes for chicken and veal stock used in the recipes. Homemade stock adds a depth of flavor to a dish not possible with canned broth. However, if time is a factor, use canned broth, buying those brands that are labeled "low sodium." Do not use diluted bouillon cubes; they are excessively salty.

CHICKEN STOCK

MAKES ABOUT 4 CUPS
PREPARATION TIME: ABOUT 40 MINUTES
COOKING TIME: ABOUT 2 HOURS AND 30 MINUTES

2 quarts (8 cups) water
2 chicken carcasses, cut in small pieces
3 onions, chopped
1 carrot, chopped
2 ribs celery, chopped
3 sprigs fresh thyme
3 sprigs fresh parsley
1 bay leaf
1 tablespoon white peppercorns

1 In a large saucepan or stockpot, combine the water and chopped carcasses. Bring to a simmer over medium heat and skim the surface of any foam.

2 Add the onions, carrots, celery, thyme, parsley, bay leaf, and peppercorns. Bring to a boil, reduce the heat, and simmer for 1½ to 2 hours, skimming fat and foam from the surface as necessary, until reduced to 4 cups.

3 Pour the stock into a fine sieve and strain, extracting as much liquid as possible. Discard the solids. Cool to tepid quickly by plunging the stockpot into a sinkful of ice, cover, and refrigerate for 6 hours, until all fat particles have risen to the top. Spoon off solidified fat and discard. To use, heat the stock over medium-high heat for about 30 minutes. Adjust the seasonings and use as directed in recipe.

4 To store, cool to tepid, cover, and refrigerate for 2 to 3 days, or freeze in 1-cup quantities (for ease of use) for up to 3 months.

VEAL STOCK

MAKES ABOUT 3 QUARTS
PREPARATION TIME: ABOUT 40 MINUTES
COOKING TIME: ABOUT 7 HOURS

¼ cup plus 2 tablespoons vegetable oil
4 pounds veal marrow bones, cut into 2-inch pieces
3 onions, quartered
1 carrot, chopped
1 rib celery, chopped
1 tomato, quartered
1 bay leaf
1 tablespoon black peppercorns
2 sprigs fresh thyme
3 cloves garlic, crushed
Approximately 1 gallon (16 cups) water

1 Preheat the oven to 450 degrees F.

2 Using ¼ cup of oil, lightly oil the bones. Spread the bones in a single layer in a large roasting pan. Roast the bones, turning occasionally, for 20 minutes, or until bones are dark golden brown on all sides.

3 Transfer the bones to a large saucepan or stockpot. Add the remaining 2 tablespoons of the oil to the roasting pan and stir in the onions, carrot, celery, and tomato. Set over

medium-high heat and cook, stirring frequently, for about 15 minutes, until well browned.

4 With a slotted spoon, transfer the vegetables to the stockpot. Add the bay leaf, peppercorns, thyme, and garlic.

5 Pour off the fat from the roasting pan and discard. Set pan over medium heat and deglaze it with 2 cups water, scraping up any particles sticking to the bottom. Add this liquid to the stockpot, Then add enough additional water to cover the bones by 2 inches, and bring to a boil. Reduce the heat and let the stock barely simmer, uncovered, for 6 hours, skimming fat and foam from the surface as necessary. Let cool by plunging stockpot into a sinkful of ice cubes. Chill in the refrigerator for 12 hours, or overnight.

6 Pour the stock through a fine sieve into a clean pan. Discard the solids. Spoon off any trace of fat. Place stockpot over high heat and bring stock to a rolling boil. Lower heat and simmer for 30 minutes, or until flavor is full-bodied and liquid has slightly reduced. Use as directed in the recipe.

7 To store, cool in an ice bath, cover, and refrigerate for 2 to 3 days or freeze in 1-cup quantities (for ease of use) for up to 3 months.

De GUSTIBUS PRESENTS
THE GREAT COOKS' COOKBOOKS

Rustic Italian Cooking

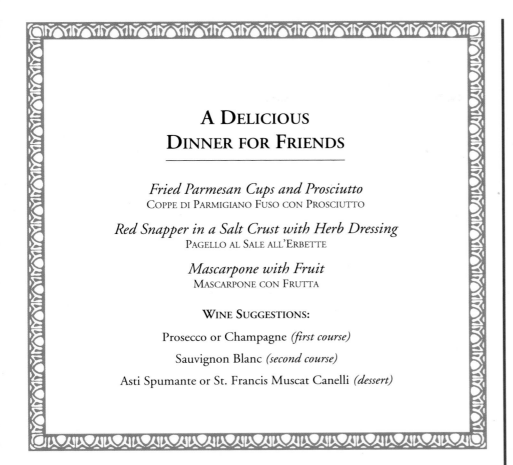

A DELICIOUS DINNER FOR FRIENDS

Fried Parmesan Cups and Prosciutto
COPPE DI PARMIGIANO FUSO CON PROSCIUTTO

Red Snapper in a Salt Crust with Herb Dressing
PAGELLO AL SALE ALL'ERBETTE

Mascarpone with Fruit
MASCARPONE CON FRUTTA

WINE SUGGESTIONS:

Prosecco or Champagne *(first course)*

Sauvignon Blanc *(second course)*

Asti Spumante or St. Francis Muscat Canelli *(dessert)*

WHAT YOU CAN PREPARE AHEAD OF TIME

Early in the day Make the Fried Parmesan Cups. Store at room temperature in a dry spot. (If the day is very humid, do not make these ahead of time.) Prepare the Red Snapper for baking. Stuff it with the herbs and garlic and wrap in plastic wrap. Refrigerate until ready to lay in the salt and bake.

Francesco Antonucci first taught at De Gustibus when he was at the Remi restaurant on Manhattan's East Side. His food was so outstanding and the restaurant so popular that he was forced to move to larger premises across town on the West Side. The crowds and the kudos followed!

When Chef Antonucci teaches, he always keeps the home kitchen in mind. Even though his food is very sophisticated, home cooks find it easy to prepare. This particular menu was wildly popular—each course had the classroom shouting "More!" The Parmesan Cups add a crispy, savory crunch to the beginning of the meal (and lend themselves to a variety of other uses). And wait until you bring the red snapper to the table—your guests will be impressed by this special dish that is as dramatic as it is delicious. The snapper will be the highlight of the dinner party, and so we have decided to end the meal in a typically Italian fashion: wonderful cheese and beautifully ripe fruit.

◁ FRANCESCO ANTONUCCI: **Mascarpone with Fruit (recipe on page 21)**

Fried Parmesan Cups and Prosciutto

Coppe di Parmigiano Fuso con Prosciutto

Once you get the knack of these cups, you'll make them regularly. The rich cheese taste is completely unadulterated and quite addictive! For success in creating these gems, start with a perfectly smooth, nonstick pan and the best imported Parmigiano-Reggiano you can find.

3 cups (about ¾ pound) freshly grated Parmigiano-Reggiano cheese
18 two-and-a-half-inch-by-two-and-a-half-inch, very thin slices prosciutto (from about 6 whole slices)
6 sprigs fresh herb, such as oregano, parsley, or rosemary

■ Special Equipment: 8-to-10-inch nonstick skillet or griddle; 3 to 6 custard cups

1 Assemble the *mise en place* trays for this recipe (see page 9). Position 3 to 6 six-ounce custard cups upside down on a work surface. The diameter of the upturned cups should be no greater than 2 to 3 inches.

2 Heat an 8- or 10-inch nonstick skillet or small, smooth griddle over medium heat for about 5 minutes, until very hot. Sprinkle 2 tablespoons of the grated cheese into the center of the pan and, gently shaking the pan in a back-and-forth motion or spreading the cheese with a spatula, evenly distribute it to form a thin, lacy circle. Cook for 30 seconds, or until the cheese has melted and turned pale golden. (Do not turn the cheese circles over.) Using a spatula, carefully lift the cheese circle and place onto an inverted cup, letting it bend down over the sides of the cup. Allow to cool completely and harden before gently lifting the cheese cup off the custard cup. Continue making cheese circles until you have at least 18 cups.

3 Arrange 3 Parmesan cups on each serving plate, rounded side up. Drape a square of prosciutto over the top of each one.
Garnish the plates with the fresh herb sprigs, and serve immediately.

▶ Three measured cups of cheese should make as many as 24 cooked Parmesan Cups. This amount allows for a couple of "practice" cups, breakage, and nibbling.

▶ If the air is humid, the cups may collapse if made in advance and left at room temperature. Even slight humidity will make them chewy.

▷ FRANCESCO ANTONUCCI: Fried Parmesan Cups and Prosciutto

Red Snapper in a Salt Crust with Herb Dressing

SERVES 6
PREPARATION TIME: ABOUT 15 MINUTES
COOKING TIME: ABOUT 60 MINUTES

Pagello al Sale all'Erbette

The salt crust sounds overpowering but in actuality it holds in moisture while imparting a delicate and pleasing salty flavor. You can use this method to cook any whole fish with scales. Splash a bit of citrus on before serving to heighten the flavor even more. This is wonderful with sautéed greens.

SNAPPER:

1 bunch fresh rosemary, rinsed and patted dry
1 bunch fresh sage, rinsed and patted dry
1 bunch fresh thyme, rinsed and patted dry
3 cloves garlic
2 three-to-four-pound red snappers or 1 six-to-eight-pound red snapper, scales, skin, and tail intact, rinsed and patted dry
4 pounds coarse sea salt or kosher salt
¼ cup all-purpose flour
2 tablespoons water

HERB DRESSING:

Juice of ½ lemon
Salt and freshly ground white pepper to taste
1 cup extra-virgin olive oil
½ cup water
1 teaspoon minced fresh rosemary
1 teaspoon minced fresh flat-leaf parsley
1 teaspoon dried oregano
½ teaspoon minced garlic

1 Preheat the oven to 400 degrees F. Assemble the *mise en place* trays for this recipe (see page 9).

2 Divide each bunch of herbs into 4 equal portions. Combine these portions to make 4 bunches of mixed herbs. Using kitchen twine, tie each bunch together. Place 2 bunches of herbs and 1½ cloves of garlic in the cavity of each fish. If using 1 fish, make 2 bunches of herbs and put all 3 cloves of garlic in the cavity.

FRANCESCO ANTONUCCI: **Red Snapper in a Salt Crust with Herb Dressing**

3 In a large bowl, combine the sea salt, flour, and water. Mix to make a rough dough. Spread evenly in a 3-inch-deep baking pan large enough to hold the fish flat. Lay the fish in the center of the salt mixture and generously cover them with salt mixture gathered up from the sides of the pan, patting the mixture firmly with your fingertips to help it adhere. Bake, uncovered, for 1 hour. (As it bakes the salt will form a compact crust.)

4 Meanwhile, make the dressing. In a small bowl, combine the lemon juice and salt and white pepper to taste.

Slowly whisk in the olive oil. When emulsified, whisk in the water, minced fresh herbs, oregano, and garlic.

5 Remove the fish from the oven. Gently crack the salt crust open and carefully remove the crust along with the fish skin. Use kitchen shears to cut through the crust and skin, if necessary. Brush any loose salt off the fish. Using 2 spatulas, lift the fish onto a warm serving platter. Pour the herb dressing over the top, and serve immediately.

▶ **For a more elaborate Italian dinner, serve pasta before the fish course and a simple grilled poultry or meat afterwards. Vegetables can be served as a separate course or with the main course.**

Mascarpone with Fruit

Mascarpone con Frutta

Mascarpone is a double-to-triple-cream cow's milk cheese from Italy's Lombardy region, and frequently sweetened and served with fresh or dried fruit as a dessert. It ranges in texture from very soft, almost runny, to the consistency of room-temperature cream cheese or butter. Its delicate flavor blends well with a wide variety of both savory and sweet seasonings. A small portion of rich, buttery mascarpone requires only a piece of sweet fruit as enrichment to make a most satisfying dessert.

3/4 pound mascarpone cheese
6 ripe large fruits, such as peaches, pears, or apples
12 ripe, small fruits, such as figs, apricots, or small bunches of grapes, or an assortment of dried fruits

Place the mascarpone cheese on a platter. Serve it with a bowl of the fruit. Let the guests peel and cut the fruit themselves.

▶ **Serve whatever fruit is in season, either by the piece or in a large, overflowing centerpiece, allowing your guests to choose whatever they wish.**

▶ **For the best mascarpone, buy the cheese from a cheese shop or an Italian market.**

▶ **Instead of fresh fruit, you can serve dried fruit. Or bring white wine or water seasoned with pungent spices to a boil and pour this over the dried fruit. Let it soak for at least 8 hours. The soaking gives the fruit time to absorb the flavors of the wine or spiced water and to plump up.**

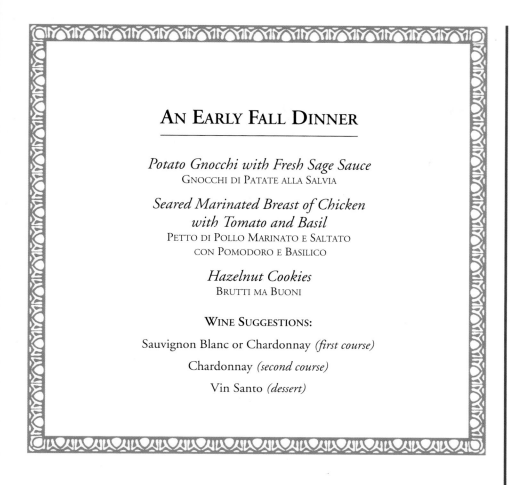

AN EARLY FALL DINNER

Potato Gnocchi with Fresh Sage Sauce
GNOCCHI DI PATATE ALLA SALVIA

*Seared Marinated Breast of Chicken
with Tomato and Basil*
PETTO DI POLLO MARINATO E SALTATO
CON POMODORO E BASILICO

Hazelnut Cookies
BRUTTI MA BUONI

WINE SUGGESTIONS:

Sauvignon Blanc or Chardonnay *(first course)*

Chardonnay *(second course)*

Vin Santo *(dessert)*

WHAT YOU CAN PREPARE AHEAD OF TIME

Up to 1 week ahead: Prepare the Chicken Stock (if making your own). Bake the Hazelnut Cookies. Store tightly covered in an airtight container in a cool place. Make and freeze the Potato Gnocchi. Do not thaw before cooking; add 2 to 4 minutes to the cooking time.

The day before: Marinate the chicken for the Seared Breast of Chicken.

Early in the day: Make the Tomato and Basil Sauce for the Seared Breast of Chicken, up to the point of adding the basil. Reheat over low heat and add the basil just before serving.

Up to 3 hours before: Make the Fresh Sage Sauce. Keep warm in the top half of a double boiler over hot water.

Up to 1 1/2 hours before: Make the gnocchi and allow to stand at room temperature until ready to cook (if not already made and frozen).

Lidia Bastianich is the epitome of earth mother. When she teaches at De Gustibus, we are all embraced by her warmth. She has great knowledge of the history, the chemistry, and the taste of food and combines her understanding with a caring empathy with the home cook.

Chef Bastianich grew up on a farm in Istria, Italy, where she learned to cook. Her simple origins meshed with her intellectual curiosity have translated into a teaching style that keeps the classroom mesmerized. In the menu we have chosen, you can really taste each ingredient, providing the cook with a more complete understanding of Lidia's style of cooking. Many of the dishes can be prepared in advance, which makes for a very relaxing evening with friends.

◁ LIDIA BASTIANICH: Hazelnut Cookies (recipe on page 27)

Potato Gnocchi with Fresh Sage Sauce

Gnocchi di Patate alla Salvia

Gnocchi are Italian dumplings made from flour, farina, or, as in this case, potatoes. Sometimes they are made with the addition of either eggs and cheese, or both. When Lidia makes them, they are silky and light as a feather. With her recipe, yours should be also.

6 large Idaho or russet potatoes, peeled and cut into quarters
2 large eggs, beaten
1 tablespoon salt
Freshly ground white pepper to taste
About 4 cups sifted, unbleached all-purpose flour
Fresh Sage Sauce (recipe follows)
1 cup freshly grated Parmigiano-Reggiano cheese

1 Assemble the *mise en place* trays for this recipe (see page 9).

2 Place the potatoes in a large saucepan with enough cold water to cover by several inches. Bring to a boil over high heat, lower the heat, and simmer for 15 minutes, or until tender. Drain well. Push the potatoes through a ricer or a food mill into a medium-sized bowl, or mash with an old-fashioned potato masher and allow to cool thoroughly, about 30 minutes.

3 Mound the potatoes on a cool work surface, such as a marble slab. Make a well in the center, and add the beaten eggs, 1 teaspoon of the salt, and white pepper to taste. Using both hands, work the mixture together, slowly adding 3 cups flour. Scrape the dough up from the surface with a pastry scraper or knife and keep blending until you have a smooth dough that is still sticky on the inside. The whole process should take no longer than 10 minutes (the more you work this dough, the more flour it absorbs). Sprinkle the dough with a little flour.

4 Cut the dough into 8 equal pieces. Sprinkle your hands with flour and using both hands, roll each piece on a lightly floured surface into a 1/2-inch-thick rope, continuously sprinkling flour on the work surface and your hands as you work the dough. Cut each rope into 1/2-inch pieces and set the pieces on an ungreased baking sheet. Indent each gnocchi with your thumb or score with the tines of fork. (The texture on the gnocchi will help the sauce adhere.)

5 Meanwhile, bring a 6-quart saucepan of water to a boil over high heat. Just as it comes to a boil, add the remaining 2 teaspoons salt.

6 Drop the gnocchi into the boiling water a few at a time, stirring the water continuously with a wooden spoon. Boil for 2 to 3 minutes, until the gnocchi rise to the top. Using a slotted spoon, transfer the gnocchi to a warm serving platter. Let the water return to a boil before adding each new batch of gnocchi.

7 Pour the Fresh Sage Sauce over the gnocchi, stir in the grated cheese and pepper to taste, and serve immediately.

■ **Special Equipment: Potato ricer, food mill, or old-fashioned potato masher**

FRESH SAGE SAUCE
Salsa alla Salvia

MAKES ABOUT 4 CUPS

1 cup unsalted butter
8 to 10 large fresh sage leaves, quartered
2 cups heavy cream
1 cup Chicken Stock (page 13)
Salt and freshly ground white pepper to taste

In a medium-sized saucepan, melt the butter over medium heat. Add the sage and sauté for 2 minutes. Stir in the cream and stock, bring to a simmer, and simmer for 5 minutes. Season to taste with salt and pepper. Serve warm.

▶ **Although the sauce is not particularly thick when it's finished, it thickens nicely when mixed with the potato gnocchi and the grated cheese.**

▷ LIDIA BASTIANICH: **Potato Gnocchi with Fresh Sage Sauce**

Seared Marinated Breast of Chicken with Tomato and Basil

SERVES 6
PREPARATION TIME: ABOUT 40 MINUTES
COOKING TIME: ABOUT 25 MINUTES
MARINATING TIME: AT LEAST 8 HOURS

Petto di Pollo Marinato e Saltato Con Pomodoro e Basilico

Simple but full of flavor, this dish is a home cook's dream. The chicken can marinate overnight and the sauce can be made early in the day. It could be served over pasta for a less formal meal, or at room temperature for an easy summer lunch.

MARINADE AND CHICKEN:

½ cup olive oil
4 cloves garlic, crushed
1 tablespoon minced fresh rosemary
1 tablespoon minced fresh sage
Salt and freshly ground black pepper to taste
2 pounds skinless, boneless chicken breasts, split and trimmed

SAUCE:

¼ cup olive oil
8 cloves garlic, crushed
1 pound ripe plum tomatoes, cored, peeled, seeded, and thinly sliced, juices reserved
Red pepper flakes to taste
Salt and freshly ground black pepper to taste
½ cup shredded fresh basil leaves

1 Assemble the *mise en place* trays for the marinade and chicken (see page 9).

2 To make the marinade, in a small bowl, combine the olive oil, garlic, rosemary, sage, and salt and pepper to taste.

3 Slice the chicken breasts on the diagonal into thirds. Using a large knife or cleaver, lightly pound each piece to flatten slightly. Place in a shallow glass or ceramic dish. Pour the marinade over the chicken, cover, and refrigerate for at least 8 hours, turning occasionally.

4 Assemble the *mise en place* trays for the sauce (see page 9).

5 To make the sauce, in a medium-sized saucepan, heat 3 tablespoons of the olive oil over moderate heat. Add the garlic and sauté for about 4 minutes, or until lightly browned. Stir in the tomatoes with their juices, the red

LIDIA BASTIANICH: **Seared Marinated Breast of Chicken with Tomato and Basil**

pepper flakes, and salt and pepper to taste. Simmer for 5 minutes. Stir in half of the basil leaves. Remove from the heat and cover to keep warm.

6 Heat a large sauté pan over medium-high heat until very hot. Drain the chicken, discarding the marinade. Add the chicken to the hot pan, without crowding, and sauté for 5 to 10 minutes, or until golden brown on both sides and just cooked through. (Cook the chicken in batches or in 2 pans if necessary.) Transfer to a large, warm serving platter.

7 Drizzle the remaining 1 tablespoon olive oil over the tomato sauce and pour over the chicken. Sprinkle the remaining basil over the top and serve.

Hazelnut Cookies

Brutti ma Buoni

Here is a simple cookie to dip into Vin Santo or a frothy cappuccino. These are good keepers, so make a couple of batches to have on hand.

1 cup finely chopped toasted and skinned hazelnuts (see page 12)
1 cup confectioners' sugar, sifted
1/8 teaspoon ground cinnamon
4 large egg whites

1 Assemble the *mise en place* trays for this recipe (see page 9). Preheat the oven to 400 degrees F. Line 2 baking sheets with parchment paper.

2 In a heavy saucepan, combine the nuts, confectioners' sugar, and cinnamon.

3 In a large bowl, using an electric mixer set on medium-high speed, beat the egg whites until stiff. Gently stir the whites into the nut mixture. Cook over medium heat, stirring constantly, for 8 to 10 minutes, or until golden brown and the mixture pulls away from the sides of the pan. Remove from the heat.

4 Using 2 teaspoons, scoop out rough 1 1/2- to 2-inch mounds of the mixture and place them about 1 1/2 inches apart on the prepared baking sheets. Bake for 10 minutes, or until lightly browned. Lifting the paper by both ends, transfer the cookies, still on the paper, to a wire rack to cool and set. Repeat with the other sheet of parchment paper.

5 Lift the cookies from the paper with a spatula. Store, tightly covered, until ready to serve.

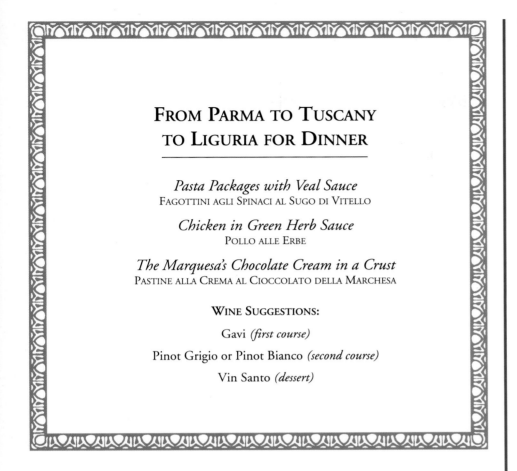

From Parma to Tuscany
to Liguria for Dinner

Pasta Packages with Veal Sauce
FAGOTTINI AGLI SPINACI AL SUGO DI VITELLO

Chicken in Green Herb Sauce
POLLO ALLE ERBE

The Marquesa's Chocolate Cream in a Crust
PASTINE ALLA CREMA AL CIOCCOLATO DELLA MARCHESA

WINE SUGGESTIONS:

Gavi *(first course)*

Pinot Grigio or Pinot Bianco *(second course)*

Vin Santo *(dessert)*

WHAT YOU CAN PREPARE AHEAD OF TIME

Up to 1 week ahead: Prepare the Chicken or Veal Stock (if making your own).

Up to 3 days ahead: Make the Veal Sauce for the Pasta Packages. Cover and refrigerate. Reheat just before serving.

Up to 1 day ahead: Cook the Chicken in Green Herb Sauce. Cover and refrigerate. Reheat, covered with foil, in a preheated 325 degree F. oven for 20 minutes before serving.

Early in the day: Assemble the Pasta Packages up to the addition of the balsamella sauce. Cover and refrigerate the pasta and balsamella sauce separately. Remove from the refrigerator 1 hour before baking, and whisk the sauce before pouring it over the pasta. Make the Chocolate Cream. Bake the cookie shells for the Chocolate Cream. Store in a cool, dry place. Assemble The Marquesa's Chocolate Cream in a Crust at least 30 minutes before serving.

Giuliano Bugialli is the De Gustibus Grand Master of Italian cooking. Over the years, he has introduced us to the art of preparing authentic and historically correct Italian meals. The admiration we all feel for his professional quest just grows and grows.

Always dazzled by Chef Bugialli's fresh pasta, veteran students are still attempting to recreate the perfectly light pasta texture at which he excels. Since much of this menu can be prepared in advance, your travels through Italy shouldn't be too tiring. Giuliano is a cook who prefers recipes in their classic form, so you should feel a real sense of accomplishment when you offer this meal.

◁ GIULIANO BUGIALLI: **Pasta Packages with Veal Sauce (recipe on page 30)**

Pasta Packages with Veal Sauce

Fagottini agli Spinaci al Sugo di Vitello

This deliciously rich pasta dish comes from Parma. It is not for the diet-conscious, as it has many eggs, lots of cheese, and some other fat as well. However, the taste is definitely worth an occasional splurge.

VEAL SAUCE:

1 tablespoon minced garlic
1 tablespoon fresh rosemary leaves
2 tablespoons olive oil
1 four-ounce piece fatty prosciutto or pancetta, diced
1 pound veal stew meat, cut into large pieces
1/8 teaspoon freshly grated nutmeg, or to taste
Pinch of ground cinnamon
1 cup dry red wine
Salt and freshly ground black pepper to taste
3 tablespoons tomato paste
2 cups Chicken Stock or Veal stock (page 13)

BALSAMELLA SAUCE:

8 tablespoons unsalted butter
1 clove garlic, peeled
1/4 cup unbleached all-purpose flour
4 cups milk

SPINACH FILLING:

Coarse sea salt or kosher salt
2 pounds fresh spinach, tough stems removed, soaked for 30 minutes in cold water
1/4 pound ricotta cheese, very well drained (see Note)
1/2 pound mascarpone cheese
1/2 cup freshly grated Parmigiano-Reggiano cheese, plus extra for serving if desired
1 extra-large egg
3 extra-large egg yolks
Freshly grated nutmeg to taste
Salt and freshly ground black pepper to taste

PASTA:

About 2 1/4 cups unbleached all-purpose flour
4 extra-large egg yolks
Pinch of salt
1/4 cup cold water
2 tablespoons olive oil
2 tablespoons unsalted butter, at room temperature

■ Special Equipment: Meat grinder; pasta machine.

1 Assemble the *mise en place* trays for this recipe (see page 9).

2 To make the veal sauce, mash the garlic and rosemary together.

3 In a medium-sized heat-proof casserole, heat the olive oil over medium heat. Add the garlic mixture and the prosciutto and sauté for about 3 minutes, stirring constantly. Add the veal and sauté for about 5 minutes, or until lightly golden. Season with nutmeg and cinnamon and mix well. Add the wine, bring to a simmer, and simmer for about 10 minutes. Remove the casserole from the heat and strain the contents through a fine sieve. Pour the liquid back into the casserole and season to taste with salt and pepper.

4 Transfer the solids in the sieve to a meat grinder and finely grind into a bowl. Add the ground meat to liquid in the casserole and return to medium heat.

5 Whisk together the tomato paste and 1 cup of the stock. Add this to the casserole. Bring to a simmer, cover, and simmer for at least 1 hour, adding additional broth as needed, until the sauce is reduced and quite thick. Taste and adjust the seasoning with salt and pepper. You should have about 3 cups of sauce. Set the sauce aside.

6 To make the balsamella sauce, melt the butter in a medium-sized saucepan over medium heat. Add the garlic and sauté for 1 minute. Remove and discard the garlic. Stir the flour into the butter to make a *roux,* and cook for 1 to 2 minutes. Whisk in the milk. Cook, whisking continuously, for 5 to 8 minutes, or until thickened. Scrape into a

bowl and place a piece of buttered waxed paper directly on the surface to prevent skin from forming. Set aside.

7 To make the spinach filling, bring a large pot of cold water to a boil over medium heat, and when the water reaches a boil, add salt to taste. Drain the spinach and add to the pot. Boil for 5 minutes, drain, and refresh under cold running water. Squeeze the spinach almost dry and finely chop. You will have about 2½ cups of loosely packed chopped spinach.

8 Combine the spinach, ricotta, mascarpone, Parmigiano, egg, and egg yolks in a bowl and mix well. Stir in the nutmeg, salt and pepper to taste. Cover and refrigerate until needed.

9 To make the pasta, mound the flour on a clean, flat work surface (preferably wood). Make a well in the center and add the egg yolks and salt.

10 Using a fork, mix the eggs and salt together and then begin to incorporate the flour by pulling it into the eggs from the inner rim of the well. Using your hands, begin incorporating more flour by pushing it under the dough that is forming to keep it from sticking to the surface. Push some of the flour aside, incorporating it only as you need it, and continue working the dough until well blended and no longer sticky. Lift the dough to the side of the work surface. Wash your hands and poke a dry finger into the dough. If it comes out clean, the dough needs no additional flour. If it comes out sticky, incorporate more flour.

11 Using a pastry scraper, clean the work surface of all flour and any caked dough bits. Place the dough on the clean surface and knead it by pushing down with the palm of one hand. Fold the dough over and continue kneading, pushing and folding, for 3 minutes and no longer than 8 minutes, until very smooth. Divide the dough into 2 or 3 pieces to make it easier to work with.

12 Using a hand-cranked pasta machine, stretch each piece of dough into sheets a little less than ¹⁄₁₆ inch thick (usually the last setting). Cut the pasta sheet into 6-inch squares.

13 In a shallow dish, combine the water and olive oil. Set aside.

14 Preheat the oven to 375 degrees F. Generously butter a 13½-inch-by-8¾-inch baking dish with the butter.

15 Bring a large saucepan of water to a boil and when it reaches a boil, add salt to taste. Cook the pasta squares in batches for 8 to 10 seconds, or until just barely firm. Using a slotted spoon, transfer the pasta to the water and oil mixture to stop further cooking. Remove the pasta squares and arrange in a single layer on clean, moistened cotton kitchen towels to rest. You should have 24 to 26 pasta squares.

16 Place 2 heaping tablespoons of the spinach filling in the center of each pasta square. Fold each one up as if you were wrapping a package: fold two sides into the center over the top of the mixture so that there is a seam; then tuck each end under. Carefully transfer to the buttered baking dish and arrange them, seam side up, in a single layer. Pour the balsamella sauce over the top. Bake for 20 minutes, or until heated through.

17 Meanwhile, reheat the veal sauce over medium-low heat for 8 to 10 minutes, stirring occasionally, until heated through.

18 Remove the baking dish from the oven and spoon the veal sauce over the pasta packages. Serve immediately, with additional grated Parmigiano, if desired.

NOTE: To drain ricotta, place it in a fine sieve set over a bowl. Allow to drain for 1 hour before using.

▶ You can replace the homemade pasta with commercially made pasta sheets, although most commercially made pasta sheets are not as thin as homemade ones.

Chicken in Green Herb Sauce

Pollo alle Erbe

An interesting chicken recipe from Tuscany, using the underutilized leg and thigh meat. The intense, fresh herb taste permeates the flavorful meat for a complex yet simple-to-prepare dish.

1½ ounces (2 to 3 slices) white bread, crusts removed
7 tablespoons fresh rosemary leaves
45 large fresh sage leaves
3 large cloves garlic, peeled
7 tablespoons Chicken Stock (page 13)
6 tablespoons olive oil
6 boneless chicken legs, skin on, trimmed of excess fat (from 3½-pound chickens, if possible)
6 boneless chicken thighs, skin on, trimmed of excess fat (from 3½-pound chickens, if possible)
Salt and freshly ground black pepper to taste
1 cup dry white wine
2 scant tablespoons fresh lemon juice
Grated zest of 2 lemons

1 Preheat the oven to 250 degrees F. Assemble the *mise en place* trays for this recipe (see page 9).

2 In a food processor fitted with the metal blade, combine the bread, rosemary, sage, garlic, and stock and pulse until finely ground. Set aside.

3 In a large sauté pan, heat the oil over low heat. Add the chicken, increase the heat to medium, and cook for about 15 minutes, turning once, until lightly golden on both sides and the juices run clear when the meat is pierced with the tip of a knife. Remove the pan from the heat. Season the chicken with salt and pepper to taste, and transfer to a large, ovenproof serving platter. Cover with aluminum foil and put in the oven to keep warm.

4 Scrape the bread and herb mixture into the sauté pan, and season with salt and pepper. Set the pan over medium heat and cook the mixture for about 4 minutes, continuously scraping the bottom of the pan with a wooden spoon. Combine the wine and lemon juice and pour into the pan. Cook for about 3 minutes, stirring continuously to deglaze the pan and make a smooth sauce. Strain the sauce through a fine sieve into a bowl, pushing on the solids with the back of a wooden spoon; discard the solids. Taste and adjust the seasonings. Pour the sauce over the chicken and sprinkle the lemon zest over all. Serve immediately.

▶ **To grate the lemon peel (or any citrus fruit) with ease, Chef Bugialli suggests covering the side of a grater with a piece of parchment paper. Rubbing the citrus fruit back and forth, turn the fruit as the peel is scraped off. Lift the parchment paper off the grater. Instead of being stuck in the grater, the tiny bits of peel remain on the paper and can be scraped into a bowl. The unwanted, bitter, white pith is left behind.**

▷ GIULIANO BUGIALLI: **Chicken in Green Herb Sauce**

The Marquesa's Chocolate Cream in a Crust

SERVES 6
PREPARATION TIME: ABOUT 1 HOUR
COOKING TIME: ABOUT 30 MINUTES
CHILLING TIME (CHOCOLATE CREAM AND FILLED MOLDS):
ABOUT 1 HOUR TOTAL

Pastine alla Crema al Cioccolato della Marchesa

A spectacularly delicious chocolate dessert from Liguria— and all the components can be made in advance.

COOKIE MOLDS:

2 extra-large egg whites
1 cup confectioners' sugar
¼ cup plus 2 tablespoons sifted, unbleached all-purpose flour
¼ cup milk
1 teaspoon pure orange extract

CHOCOLATE CREAM:

2 ounces bittersweet chocolate, coarsely chopped
8 tablespoons unsalted butter, cut into pieces, at room temperature
1 tablespoon unflavored gelatin
¼ cup cold water
¾ cup hot milk
1 tablespoon brandy
5 extra-large eggs, separated
¼ cup plus 1 tablespoon granulated sugar
2 tablespoons confectioners' sugar
½ cup bittersweet chocolate shavings (page 13)

1 Preheat the oven to 400 degrees F. Assemble the *mise en place* trays for this recipe (see page 9). Butter 4 baking sheets. Set 6 four-ounce custard cups on a work surface.

2 To make the cookie molds, using a fork, lightly beat the egg whites in a small bowl until foamy. Sift the confectioners' sugar over the whites, mixing with a wooden spoon until the sugar is completely absorbed. Add the flour a tablespoon at a time, mixing with the wooden spoon until incorporated. Combine the milk and orange extract, and stir into the batter until well blended.

3 For each cookie mold, spoon 1 tablespoon of batter onto a prepared baking sheet to form a thin circle about 5 inches in diameter. Place only 3 or 4 circles on each sheet, allowing at least 1 inch between them so that they do not run into each other during baking. Bake 1 sheet of cookies

◁ GIULIANO BUGIALLI: The Marquesa's Chocolate Cream in a Crust

at a time for 4 to 5 minutes, or until the edges of the circles are lightly golden.

4 Using a thin-edged metal spatula, lift the cookies from the baking sheets, one at a time, and immediately fit each one into a custard cup, gently pressing it into the bottom for a neat fit. (If the cookies become too firm to mold, put the baking sheet back in the oven for about 1 minute.) Allow the cookies to cool in the cups for at least 5 minutes, or until firm, and then carefully remove them from the cups and set on a wire rack to cool completely. When cool, set on an ungreased baking sheet or tray. You will need 12 cups, and there is enough batter for a couple of practice cups.

5 To make the chocolate cream, put the chocolate in a medium-sized bowl or the top of a double boiler and melt it over very warm, but not simmering, water. Add the butter and, using a wooden spoon, beat vigorously for about 2 minutes, until well incorporated.

6 Meanwhile, in a small bowl, sprinkle the gelatin over the water. Let it soften for about 5 minutes. Add the hot milk and stir until the gelatin is completely dissolved.

7 Pour the gelatin mixture into the chocolate mixture, stirring continuously with a wooden spoon. Remove the chocolate mixture from the pan of water. Stir in the brandy and then the egg yolks, one at a time. Let cool for about 20 minutes.

8 In a large bowl, using an electric mixer set on medium-high speed, whip the egg whites until foamy. Add the granulated and confectioners' sugar and continue to beat until stiff, about 3 to 4 minutes. Gently fold the meringue into the cooled chocolate mixture. Cover and refrigerate for 30 minutes.

9 Spoon 2 heaping tablespoons of the chocolate mixture into each cooled cookie mold and refrigerate for at least 30 minutes. When ready to serve, sprinkle chocolate shavings over each filled cup.

▶ **The cookie shells do not hold up well if made on a humid day.**

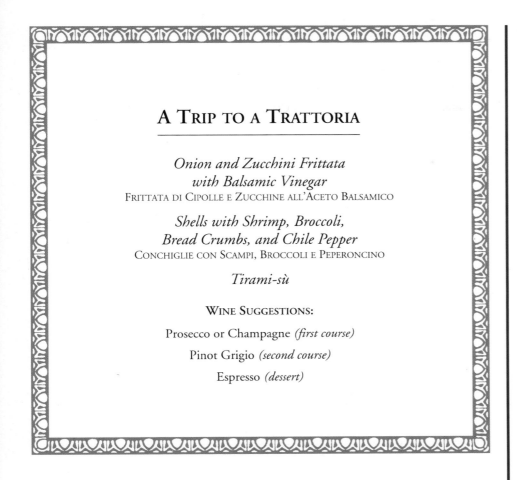

A TRIP TO A TRATTORIA

*Onion and Zucchini Frittata
with Balsamic Vinegar*
FRITTATA DI CIPOLLE E ZUCCHINE ALL'ACETO BALSAMICO

*Shells with Shrimp, Broccoli,
Bread Crumbs, and Chile Pepper*
CONCHIGLIE CON SCAMPI, BROCCOLI E PEPERONCINO

Tirami-sù

WINE SUGGESTIONS:

Prosecco or Champagne *(first course)*

Pinot Grigio *(second course)*

Espresso *(dessert)*

WHAT YOU CAN PREPARE AHEAD OF TIME

The day before: Make the Tirami-sù.

Up to 6 hours ahead: If you plan to serve it at room temperature, make the Onion and Zucchini Frittata.

Biba Caggiano lives in Sacramento, California, where she is the chef-owner of the restaurant that bears her name. She travels frequently and whenever we are able to schedule a class with her, we have a great time getting reacquainted with her no-nonsense approach to food. Practicality seems to be her middle name! Just before Biba's last class, she had visited trattorias throughout Italy and she came loaded with many of their homey Italian recipes, reworked for the American home cook.

The menu we have chosen is easy, full of flavor, and jam-packed with savory taste combinations. Especially inviting is Biba's recipe for tirami-sù, everyone's favorite Italian dessert.

◁ BIBA CAGGIANO: **Onion and Zucchini Frittata with Balsamic Vinegar on a terrace in Tuscany (recipe on page 38)**

Onion and Zucchini Frittata with Balsamic Vinegar

SERVES 6
PREPARATION TIME: ABOUT 20 MINUTES
COOKING TIME: ABOUT 25 MINUTES

Frittata di Cipolle e Zucchine all'Aceto Balsamico

A frittata is an easy-to-make Italian omelet in which the flavors are mixed into the eggs. This frittata is incredibly versatile. Try serving it at brunch or lunch as a light entrée by making individual frittatas in a nonstick five- or six-inch crêpe pan; prepare it for a picnic; or slice and serve it as an hors d'oeuvre.

9 large eggs
3/4 cup freshly grated Parmigiano-Reggiano cheese
1 1/2 tablespoons chopped fresh parsley
8 fresh basil leaves, finely shredded
Salt to taste
3 tablespoons olive oil
1 large onion, thinly sliced
2 medium zucchini, trimmed and thinly sliced
2 tablespoons balsamic vinegar

1 Assemble the *mise en place* trays for this recipe (see page 9).

2 In a medium-sized bowl, lightly beat the eggs. Stir in the Parmigiano, parsley, and basil. Season to taste with salt.

3 In a 12-inch, nonstick skillet, heat the oil over medium heat. Add the onion and cook, stirring continuously, for 3 to 5 minutes. Add the zucchini and cook, stirring, for 5 to 8 minutes, until both vegetables are lightly golden. Stir in 1 1/2 tablespoons of the balsamic vinegar and immediately remove from the heat. Using a slotted spoon, transfer the vegetables to the egg mixture, draining them against the side of the skillet and leaving what liquid there is in the pan. Mix vegetable and egg mixture well.

4 Return the skillet to medium heat and add the vegetable-egg mixture. Cook for about 6 minutes, or until the bottom of the frittata is set and lightly browned.

5 Invert a large, flat plate over the skillet and invert the frittata onto it. Slide the frittata back into the skillet and cook for 3 to 4 minutes more, until set in the center and lightly browned on the bottom. Slide the frittata onto a warm serving dish. Immediately drizzle the remaining 1/2 tablespoon balsamic vinegar over the top. Serve warm or at room temperature, cut into 6 wedges.

▶ **The amount of balsamic vinegar required really depends on the strength of the vinegar. The stronger the vinegar, the less you need to use. It's worth it to taste different brands of balsamic vinegar and choose those that you particularly like. Not all taste the same.**

▷ BIBA CAGGIANO: Onion and Zucchini Frittata with Balsamic Vinegar

Shells with Shrimp, Broccoli, Bread Crumbs, and Chile Pepper

SERVES 6
PREPARATION TIME: ABOUT 20 MINUTES
COOKING TIME: ABOUT 20 MINUTES

Conchiglie con Scampi, Broccoli, e Peperoncino

This simple seafood pasta dish requires only three-quarters of a pound of shrimp to feed six nicely—an economy that pays off handsomely in the cholesterol department, too.

2 pounds broccoli, stalks removed and florets separated
⅓ cup extra-virgin olive oil
¾ pound medium shrimp, shelled, deveined, rinsed, and well drained
2 tablespoons fresh white bread crumbs (see page 12)
4 anchovy fillets, separated from one another
3 cloves garlic, minced
Generous pinch of red pepper flakes, or more to taste
Salt to taste
1 pound dried pasta shells, orecchiette, or penne

1 Assemble the *mise en place* trays for this recipe (see page 9).

2 In a steamer basket, steam the broccoli over boiling water for 4 minutes, or until tender. Refresh under cold running water and set aside.

3 In a large skillet, heat the oil over medium heat until nearly smoking. Add the shrimp and cook, stirring continuously, for 1 to 2 minutes, or until opaque. Using a slotted spoon, transfer the shrimp to a plate.

4 Immediately stir the bread crumbs into the skillet, and stir for 10 seconds, or until the crumbs are lightly golden. (The pan is very hot and the bread crumbs will brown in no time at all.) Stir in the anchovies and garlic. Cook for 15 to 20 seconds, stirring, until the garlic is browned and cooked. Return the shrimp to the skillet and add the broccoli florets and red pepper flakes. Season to taste with salt and cook, stirring continuously, for 1 minute. Remove from the heat.

5 Bring a large pot of water to a boil. When it boils, add salt and cook the pasta for about 10 minutes, or until *al dente*. Drain well, reserving some of the cooking water.

6 Add the pasta to the skillet and set over medium heat. Cook for 1 to 2 minutes, stirring continuously, until the pasta, shrimp, and vegetables are well combined. If the pasta looks dry, add 2 to 3 tablespoons of the reserved cooking water. Taste and adjust the seasoning with salt and red pepper flakes. Serve immediately.

▶ **If you have organized your *mise en place* well, this recipe will come together in minutes.**

◁ BIBA CAGGIANO: **Shells with Shrimp, Broccoli, Bread Crumbs, and Chile Pepper**

Tirami-sù

Tirami-sù, literally translated as "pick me up," needs no introduction. In the last ten years, this dessert has become more popular in America than in Italy. It is served in one version or another in all types of restaurants. Apparently, the dessert originated in Tuscany in the early 1900s, but many regions claim it as their own.

A true tirami-sù is always made with mascarpone, a delicious, sweet, soft Italian cheese, not unlike a very thick, slightly acidic whipped cream—never with any other cheese or with whipped cream.

Biba's generously portioned recipe is based on a tirami-sù from the fancy Osteria Trattoria Laguna in Cavallino, near Venice, Italy, which she found had a particular extra-light texture that made it simply irresistible. She uses a creamy zabaglione as the custard to avoid using uncooked eggs.

ZABAGLIONE:

8 large egg yolks
1/2 cup granulated sugar
1/3 cup brandy

FILLING AND CAKE:

1 1/2 pounds mascarpone cheese
4 large egg whites
2 tablespoons granulated sugar
2 cups Italian espresso, at room temperature
1/4 cup brandy
40 high-quality ladyfingers, preferably imported from Italy
1/2 cup unsweetened cocoa powder
1/2 cup semisweet chocolate curls, optional (see page 12)

1 Assemble the *mise en place* trays for this recipe (see page 9).

2 To make the zabaglione, put the egg yolks and sugar in a large bowl or the top of a double boiler set over slowly simmering water. Beat with a whisk or hand-held electric mixer set at medium speed until thick and pale yellow. Beat in the brandy and cook for about 10 minutes, whisk-ing constantly, until the zabaglione doubles in volume, is soft and fluffy, and feels hot to the touch. Immediately set the zabaglione over a bowl of ice water and let cool.

3 To make the filling, combine the mascarpone and the cooled zabaglione in the bowl of an electric mixer and beat at low speed to blend.

4 In a large bowl, using clean beaters, beat the egg whites on medium-high speed until foamy. Add the sugar and beat until stiff peaks form. Fold the egg whites into the mascarpone mixture.

5 In a medium-sized bowl, combine the espresso and brandy. One at a time, quickly dip half the ladyfingers into the coffee mixture. Lay them very close together in a 13-by-9-inch baking dish. Spread half the mascarpone mixture evenly over the ladyfingers.

6 Using a fine-mesh strainer, sprinkle half the cocoa powder evenly over the mascarpone. Dip the remaining ladyfingers in the espresso mixture and place side by side on the mascarpone, making another layer. Spread the remaining mascarpone mixture evenly over the ladyfingers, and sprinkle with the remaining cocoa powder. Cover the dish with plastic wrap and refrigerate for at least 4 hours, or overnight.

7 Just before serving, sprinkle semisweet chocolate curls over the tirami-sù, if desired.

▶ **American ladyfingers are more spongy than their Italian counterpart, and since real Italian tirami-sù requires a slightly harder cookie, Biba suggests using ladyfingers imported from Italy.**

▷ BIBA CAGGIANO: **Tirami-sù**

42

A TASTE OF TUSCANY

Noodle Tart
CROSTATA DI FETTUCCINE

Squab with Juniper Berries
PICCIONI AL GINEPRO

Cream with Amaretti
CREMA AGLI AMARETTI

WINE SUGGESTIONS:

Champagne *(first course)*

Red Bordeaux *(second course)*

Amaretto or Vin Santo *(dessert)*

WHAT YOU CAN PREPARE AHEAD OF TIME

Early in the day: Make the Noodle Tart. Reheat in a preheated 300 degree F. oven for about 10 minutes. Prepare the mushroom mixture for the Squab with Juniper Berries. Cover and refrigerate. Remove from the refrigerator 1 hour before using.

Prepare the pears and the amaretti cream for the Cream with Amaretti. Cover and refrigerate separately.

When Lorenza De'Medici taught at De Gustibus, it was like having a piece of history come alive in our kitchen. She lives in Tuscany on the family estate, Badia a Coltibuono, which is famous for both its olive oil and its wine. The recipes that she shared with us had been passed down through many generations of De'Medici cooks. Lorenza has adapted these recipes to contemporary tastes, and our students found them as inviting as a fall season in the Tuscan countryside.

◁ Dining al fresco in Montemerano, Italy

Noodle Tart

Crostata di Fettuccine

This is a somewhat unexpected way to eat pasta and cheese, but delicious nonetheless. You could also serve it as a wonderful breakfast, brunch, or lunch main course.

3 cups all-purpose flour
13 tablespoons butter, cut into pieces, at room temperature
2 large egg yolks
1/4 cup water
7 ounces dried strand noodles (not egg noodles), such as fettuccine
1/2 cup heavy cream
1/2 cup freshly grated Parmigiano-Reggiano cheese
Pinch of freshly grated nutmeg
3 ounces ham, chopped (see note)
Salt and freshly ground black pepper to taste

■ Special Equipment: 9-inch fluted tart pan with removable bottom; pastry weights, beans, or rice

1 Preheat the oven to 375 degrees F. Assemble the *mise en place* trays for this recipe (see page 9). Generously butter and flour a 9-inch fluted tart pan with a removable bottom.

2 In a food processor fitted with the metal blade, combine the flour, 10 tablespoons of the butter, the egg yolks, and water. Process until the dough pulls away from the sides of the bowl and forms a ball. Flatten the ball of dough slightly, wrap it in plastic wrap, and refrigerate for 30 minutes.

3 Roll the dough out between two sheets of plastic wrap to a circle about 11 1/2 inches in diameter and 1/4-inch thick. Fit into the prepared tart pan. Place a piece of aluminum foil over the pastry, and cover with pastry weights, dried beans, or rice.

4 Bake the tart shell for 40 minutes. Remove from the oven and lift out the weights and foil. (Leave the oven on.) Set the tart shell aside.

5 Bring a large pot of water to a boil. When the water boils, salt it lightly. Cook the pasta for about 5 minutes, or until *al dente*. Drain well and transfer to a bowl.

6 Add the remaining 3 tablespoons butter, the cream, cheese, nutmeg, and ham to the pasta, and toss to mix. Season to taste with salt and pepper. Pour the mixture into the baked tart shell. Bake for 15 minutes, or until the filling is set. Remove from the oven and carefully remove the sides of the tart pan. Place the tart on a serving platter, cut into wedges, and serve warm.

NOTE: Although any ham works well in this recipe, Prosciutto di Parma and prosciutto are good choices as they are authentic Italian hams. Like some ham, these can be salty, and you may find you need no salt at all in the recipe. High-quality prosciutto is not particularly salty.

▶ **A good way to remove the sides of the tart pan is to set the tart on a small bowl and let the sides drop away from the pie shell.**

◁ LORENZA DE'MEDICI: **Noodle Tart**

Roast Squab with Juniper Berries

Piccioni al Ginepro

This succulent squab dish is simple to prepare, easy to serve, and quick to disappear at the table. Intense flavors of juniper, porcini, and vin santo combine to say "Tuscany."

1/2 cup dried porcini mushrooms, soaked in warm water for 30 minutes
3 ounces mortadella, chopped
1 tablespoon juniper berries, crushed
1 cup freshly grated Parmigiano-Reggiano cheese
1/2 cup fine dried bread crumbs
3 tablespoons milk
1 large egg
1/2 cup vin santo or medium-dry sherry
Salt and freshly ground black pepper to taste
3 one-pound squab, rinsed and patted dry
2 tablespoons unsalted butter, melted
1 tablespoon extra-virgin olive oil

1 Preheat the oven to 350 degrees F. Assemble the *mise en place* trays for this recipe (see page 9).

2 Drain the porcini, straining and reserving the soaking water for a risotto or a soup if desired. Chop the porcini and place in a medium-sized bowl.

3 Add the mortadella and juniper berries to the porcini, and mix well. Add the Parmigiano, bread crumbs, milk, egg, and 2 tablespoons of the vin santo and mix well. Season to taste with salt and pepper.

4 Dividing the stuffing evenly among the 3 squab, spoon the stuffing into the cavities, packing firmly but not tightly. Truss the squab with kitchen twine.

5 Put the squab in a deep casserole. Brush the butter on top of the squab, and pour over the oil.

6 Cover the casserole and roast the squab for 1 hour and 30 minutes, or until they are tender and their internal temperature registers 165 degrees F. Baste the squab with the cooking juices from time to time. During the last 30 minutes of cooking, add the remaining 2 tablespoons of vin santo to the casserole.

7 Remove the squab from the casserole and remove the twine. Let the squab rest for about 10 minutes. Cut each one in half lengthwise and arrange on a warm serving platter. Strain the cooking juices over the squab and serve immediately.

▶ **Cornish game hens or small chickens (poussins) could replace the squab in this recipe.**

▶ **The porcini should be rinsed several times before soaking to remove any grit and sand.**

▶ **If you prefer, when serving, leave the squab whole and top with extra stuffing mixture.**

▷ LORENZA DE'MEDICI: **Roast Squab with Juniper Berries**

Cream with Amaretti

Crema agli Amaretti

A typical Italian dessert, this is not too sweet and includes a bit of fruit and a taste of wine—plus, it's easily made in advance!

½ cup dry white wine
½ cup water
1 bay leaf
Zest of ½ lemon
1 cup granulated sugar
6 small Bosc or other firm pears, cored from the bottom, with stems left intact
2 cups heavy cream
¼ cup Amaretto or Grand Marnier
6 Amaretti cookies, crumbled

1 Assemble the *mise en place* trays for this recipe (see page 9).

2 In a medium-sized, nonreactive saucepan, combine the wine, water, bay leaf, lemon zest, and ½ cup of the sugar. Bring to a boil over high heat. Add the pears. Cover, reduce the heat to low, and simmer for 45 minutes, or until the pears are tender when pierced with the point of a knife. Baste the pears with the poaching liquid several times during cooking. Using a slotted spoon, transfer the pears to a plate to cool.

3 Put the remaining ½ cup of sugar in a heavy-bottomed saucepan and stir constantly over medium heat until the sugar begins to foam around the edges. Continue to cook without stirring until it turns dark brown and caramelizes.

4 Meanwhile in a small saucepan, heat 1 cup of the heavy cream over low heat.

5 Using caution, stir the hot cream, a little at a time, into the caramelized sugar; it may spatter. Stir in the liqueur. Transfer to a bowl to cool completely.

6 In a medium-sized bowl, using an electric mixer set on medium-high speed, whip the remaining 1 cup cream to soft peaks. Gently fold in the liqueur-flavored cream. Cover and refrigerate until ready to serve.

7 Stand the pears upright on each individual plate and spoon the chilled cream over the pears. Sprinkle with the amaretti crumbs and serve immediately.

◁ LORENZA DE'MEDICI: **Cream with Amaretti**

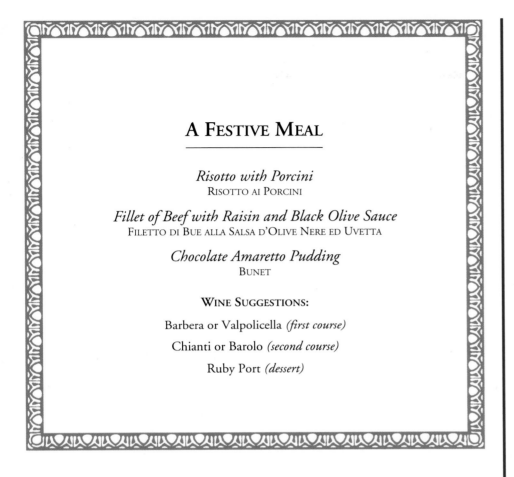

A Festive Meal

Risotto with Porcini
RISOTTO AI PORCINI

Fillet of Beef with Raisin and Black Olive Sauce
FILETTO DI BUE ALLA SALSA D'OLIVE NERE ED UVETTA

Chocolate Amaretto Pudding
BUNET

Wine Suggestions:

Barbera or Valpolicella *(first course)*

Chianti or Barolo *(second course)*

Ruby Port *(dessert)*

WHAT YOU CAN PREPARE AHEAD OF TIME

Up to 1 week ahead: Prepare the Chicken Stock (if making your own). Prepare the Veal Stock (if making your own).

Up to 3 days ahead: Make the veal reduction for the Fillet of Beef. Cover and refrigerate.

Up to 1 day ahead: Make the Chocolate Amaretto Pudding. Cover and refrigerate until ready to serve.

Early in the day: Marinate the beef and the raisins for the Fillet of Beef.

Roberto Donna came to teach at De Gustibus on the recommendation of Jean Louis Palladin of the famed Washington, D.C. restaurant, Jean-Louis at the Watergate. Jean-Louis told us that Roberto was a truly great chef who would shine in our classroom. This was no exaggeration! Roberto came, we saw, and he conquered!

The results of the menu we have chosen from Chef Donna make it worth the effort. The excitement he conveyed to his students is here in each recipe. His recipe for risotto is creamy and rich with the flavor of porcini. The contrast of the sweet raisins and tart olives offers a new dimension to the fillet of beef. And the chocolate pudding explodes with caloric goodness—it is delicious!

◁ **A home along Appia Antica, Italy**

Risotto with Porcini

Risotto ai Porcini

Risotto can be a home cook's nightmare, only because it must be made at the last minute and stirred constantly while the rice absorbs the liquid. But, with its rich, creamy taste, it's a fantastic dream to eat. And like any dream, it is worth a little effort.

1 cup Veal Stock (page 13)
6 porcini mushroom caps, wiped clean, plus 7 ounces fresh porcini mushrooms, trimmed and wiped clean
1 bulb garlic
1/4 cup olive oil
6 cups Chicken Stock (page 13)
6 tablespoons unsalted butter
1/2 large onion, minced
1/2 teaspoon minced fresh sage
1/2 teaspoon minced fresh rosemary
1 pound Arborio rice (see note)
3/4 cup dry white Italian wine, such as Pinot Grigio
Salt and freshly ground black pepper to taste

1 Preheat the oven to 375 degrees F. Assemble the *mise en place* trays for this recipe (see page 9).

2 In a small saucepan, bring the veal stock to a boil over medium heat. Reduce the heat and simmer for about 20 minutes, or until reduced to 2 tablespoons. Remove from the heat, cover, and set aside.

3 Put the porcini caps in a small baking pan. Cut the garlic bulb in half crosswise and add to the pan. Drizzle 3 tablespoons of the olive oil over the mushrooms and garlic. Set aside.

4 Cut the remaining mushrooms into 1/4-inch pieces and set aside.

5 In a medium-sized saucepan, bring the chicken stock to a simmer over medium heat. Reduce the heat to low and keep hot.

6 In a medium-sized saucepan, melt 4 tablespoons of the butter with remaining 1 tablespoon olive oil over low heat. Add the onion and cook, stirring, for about 10 minutes, or until translucent. Raise the heat to medium-high and stir in the sage, rosemary, and diced porcini. Sauté for 2 minutes. Stir in the rice, reduce the heat to medium, and toast, stirring occasionally, for 3 minutes, or until the rice is glistening. Add the wine and cook, stirring continuously, for about 1 minute, or until all the liquid has been absorbed by the rice.

7 As soon as the wine has been absorbed, begin adding the hot chicken stock to the rice 1/2 cup at a time, cooking and stirring until each addition is absorbed. This should take no more than 15 to 20 minutes, as you want the rice to be creamy but still *al dente*.

8 Meanwhile, roast the porcini caps for 10 minutes, or until just tender. Turn off the oven and open the door or remove and cover to keep warm.

9 Remove the risotto from the heat. Add the remaining 2 tablespoons butter and salt and pepper to taste, and stir until the rice is very creamy. Spoon into a warm serving bowl. If necessary, reheat the reduced veal stock. Place the porcini caps on top, and drizzle with the warm veal stock. Serve immediately.

NOTE: Arborio rice is Italian, medium-grain rice that is especially good for risotto. Buy it in specialty shops, the gourmet section of the supermarket, or an Italian grocery.

▶ **Even though risotto must be made at the last minute, this dish will all come together easily if you are well organized.**

▶ **You can buy frozen veal stock in gourmet or specialty shops.**

◁ ROBERTO DONNA: **Risotto with Porcini**

Fillet of Beef with Raisin and Black Olive Sauce

Filetto di Bue alla Salsa d'Olive Nere ed Uvetta

Profoundly concentrated flavors heighten the taste of the tender fillet. I think that this dish could also be done with pork or tender lamb loins with the same aromatic result.

4 cups Veal Stock (page 13)
1 one-and-a-half-pound beef tenderloin, trimmed and cut crosswise into 6 pieces
1/3 cup olive oil
3 cloves garlic, sliced
3 fresh rosemary sprigs
1/2 cup raisins
1/4 cup Cognac
1 tablespoon prepared black olive puree

1 Assemble the *mise en place* trays for this recipe (see page 9).

2 Put the beef in a shallow dish. Add the olive oil, garlic, and rosemary, and toss to coat. Cover with plastic wrap and refrigerate at least 2 hours.

3 Meanwhile, in a small bowl combine the raisins and Cognac. Set aside at room temperature to macerate for 2 hours.

4 In a medium-sized saucepan, simmer the veal stock over medium heat for 45 minutes to 1 hour, or until reduced to 1½ cups. Set aside.

5 Remove the beef from the marinade and pat dry with paper towel. Discard the garlic and reserve the oil and rosemary separately.

6 Drain the raisins, reserving the Cognac.

7 Preheat the oven to 175 degrees F.

8 In a large sauté pan, heat the reserved oil over high heat. Add the reserved rosemary and then add the beef and cook, turning once, for 4 to 5 minutes, until it has a nice crispy crust. Remove the rosemary from the pan as soon as it starts to darken. Add the Cognac and continue to cook for 30 seconds to 1 minute, until the Cognac has evaporated. Transfer the beef to a warm serving dish and keep warm in the oven. Spoon off any fat from the pan.

9 Add the veal reduction to the sauté pan, stir in the olive puree, and cook over medium-high heat for 2 minutes, or until reduced to a rich sauce. Stir in the raisins. Place beef on warmed dinner plates. Pour the sauce over the beef, and serve.

▶ Black olive puree, which is sometimes called olivata, is available at Italian groceries, specialty markets, and many supermarkets.

▷ ROBERTO DONNA: Fillet of Beef with Raisin and Black Olive Sauce

Chocolate Amaretto Pudding

Bunet

This rich, chocolate "bread pudding" uses delicate amaretti cookies for the bread, providing just a hint of one of Italy's favorite flavors.

10 amaretti cookies, crumbled
1½ cups granulated sugar
¼ cup unsweetened cocoa powder
6 large eggs
1 quart milk
1 cup Marsala wine
1 tablespoon plus 1 teaspoon Cognac
1 tablespoon water

1 Preheat the oven to 350 degrees F. Assemble the *mise en place* trays for this recipe (see page 9).

2 In a heatproof bowl, combine the amaretti with 1 cup plus 2 tablespoons of the sugar, the cocoa, and eggs and stir to blend.

3 In a medium-sized saucepan, bring the milk to a boil over medium heat. Immediately stir into the amaretti mixture. Stir in the Marsala and Cognac, remove from the heat, and set aside.

4 In a small saucepan, combine the water with the remaining ¼ cup plus 2 tablespoons sugar and cook over medium heat, stirring continuously, for 10 minutes, or until dark gold and caramelized. Remove from the heat and carefully pour into the bottom of a 2-quart soufflé dish or mold. Using caution, pour the milk mixture into the mold (it may splatter).

5 Place the soufflé dish into a large baking pan and add enough hot water to come about halfway up the sides of the dish. Bake for 45 minutes to 1 hour, until the center of the pudding is set. Cool completely on a wire rack. When cool, cover and refrigerate for at least 3 hours or overnight.

6 When ready to serve, place a serving plate on top of the soufflé dish and invert to unmold the pudding. Serve immediately, spooning any caramel remaining in the dish over the pudding.

▶ **Before boiling milk, wet the bottom of the saucepan with water to prevent the milk from sticking to the bottom of the pot.**

◁ ROBERTO DONNA: **Chocolate Amaretto Pudding**

Two Americans
Create "Al Forno"

Clams "Al Forno"
VONGOLE "AL FORNO"

Shells "Al Forno" with Mushrooms and Radicchio
CONCHIGLIE "AL FORNO" FUNGHI SHIITAKE E RADICCHIO

Cranberry-Walnut Tart
CROSTATA DI NOCI E CRANBERRIES

WINE SUGGESTIONS:

Pinot Grigio or Gavi *(first course)*

Sauvignon Blanc *(second course)*

Ruby Port *(dessert)*

WHAT YOU CAN PREPARE AHEAD OF TIME

Up to 1 week ahead: Make the pastry for the Cranberry Walnut Tart. Wrap tightly and freeze. Defrost, still wrapped, for 45 minutes, or until pliable but still cold.

Early in the day: Scrub the clams for the Clams "Al Forno." Prepare the Conchiglie "Al Forno." Cover and refrigerate. Bring to room temperature before baking. Bake just before serving.

Johanne and George were students at the Rhode Island School of Design when they fell in love with each other—and with the foods of Italy. They decided to forego careers in the world of design and devote their lives, together, to exploring the Italian menu. Much to the delight of lovers of great food, these two Americans have opened a great Italian restaurant in Providence, which draws diners from all over the world.

Although the dishes we have chosen from Johanne and George do not really come together as a complete menu, they each give a sense, in their recreation, of some of Italy's great recipes. And the Cranberry-Walnut Tart is perfect for the American holiday table.

◁ **Picnic on a hillside in Tuscany**

Clams "Al Forno"

Vongole "Al Forno"

This aromatic appetizer could easily be served as a main course in larger portions, with crusty bread and a tossed salad.

42 littleneck clams
1½ cups cored, peeled, seeded, and chopped ripe plum tomatoes
2 onions, halved and thinly sliced
2 tablespoons minced garlic
1 tablespoon minced jalapeño, or to taste
½ teaspoon red pepper flakes
¾ cup dry white Italian wine, such as Pinot Grigio
½ cup water
8 tablespoons unsalted butter, cut into pieces
3 scallions, trimmed and cut into 1-inch julienne
6 lemon wedges

1 Preheat the oven to 450 degrees F. Assemble the *mise en place* trays for this recipe (see page 9).

2 Wash the clams under cold running water, scrubbing them with a stiff brush. Lay in a single layer in 2 nine-by-twelve-inch shallow baking dishes. Cover with the tomatoes, onions, garlic, jalapeño, pepper flakes, wine, water, and butter.

3 Bake the clams for 6 to 7 minutes. Turn the clams and stir them to move those in the center to the sides of the pans. Bake for 10 to 15 minutes longer, or until the clams open. Discard any unopened clams.

4 Spoon the clams into shallow soup bowls. Using tongs, distribute the tomatoes and onions evenly among the bowls. Pour the broth into the bowls, sprinkle with the scallions, and garnish with the lemon wedges. Serve immediately.

▶ Although we call for more clams than you will need, to allow for any that do not open, if none stay closed, serve them all.

▶ You can use canned imported Italian plum tomatoes in place of the fresh tomatoes.

▷ JOHANNE KILLEEN AND GEORGE GERMON: Clams "Al Forno"

Shells "Al Forno" with Mushrooms and Radicchio

SERVES 6
PREPARATION TIME: ABOUT 30 MINUTES
COOKING TIME: ABOUT 45 MINUTES

Conchiglie "Al Forno" Funghi Shiitake e Radicchio

Here is a richly delicious "make ahead" casserole filled with the flavors of earthy mushrooms, sharp radicchio, and pungent cheeses. Johanne and George recommend a good imported dried pasta, such as De Cecco or Del Verde, or any pasta that is 100-percent semolina.

6 tablespoons unsalted butter
6 ounces shiitake mushrooms, wiped clean, stemmed and cut into 1/4-inch slices
Salt to taste
1 pound medium-sized dried conchiglie (pasta shells)
2 1/2 cups heavy cream
1/2 cup freshly grated Parmigiano-Reggiano cheese
1/2 cup shredded Bel Paese cheese
1/2 cup crumbled Gorgonzola cheese
2 heads (about 1 pound) radicchio, halved, cored, and shredded
6 fresh sage leaves, shredded

1 Preheat the oven to 450 degrees F. Assemble the *mise en place* trays for this recipe (see page 9). Generously butter a 9-inch square baking dish.

2 In a medium-sized sauté pan, melt 4 tablespoons butter over medium heat. Add the mushrooms and sauté for 5 minutes, or until tender. Add salt to taste. Remove from the heat and set aside.

3 Bring a large pot of water to a boil over high heat. When the water boils, add a little salt. Cook the pasta for about 10 minutes, until *al dente*. Drain well.

4 In a large bowl, combine the cream, Parmigiano-Reggiano, Bel Paese, Gorgonzola, mushrooms, and radicchio. Add the drained pasta and toss to combine. Add the sage leaves and season to taste with salt.

5 Transfer the pasta to the prepared dish. Dot with the remaining 2 tablespoons butter. Bake for 30 minutes, or until bubbly and golden brown on top. Serve immediately.

▶ The mushroom stems not needed for this recipe can be used to enrich soups, stocks, and sauces.

▶ Conchiglie is a shell-shaped pasta available in many sizes, from very small (generally for soup) to large (for stuffing).

▷ JOHANNE KILLEEN AND GEORGE GERMON: Conchiglie "Al Forno" with Mushrooms and Radicchio

Cranberry-Walnut Tart

Crostata di Noci e Cranberries

This easy-to-make dessert is perfect for the Thanksgiving and Christmas table. The dough is fail-safe and can be used for any tart or pie.

TART PASTRY:

2 cups unbleached, all-purpose flour
1/4 cup superfine sugar
1/2 teaspoon coarse salt
1 cup unsalted butter, cut into 1/2-inch cubes and chilled
1/4 cup ice water

FILLING:

2 cups fresh cranberries, rinsed and dried
1/2 cup chopped walnuts
2 tablespoons superfine sugar
2 tablespoons light brown sugar
2 tablespoons confectioners' sugar
1 cup whipped cream (optional)

1 Preheat the oven to 450 degrees F. Assemble the *mise en place* trays for this recipe (see page 9).

2 To make the tart pastry, combine the flour, sugar, and salt in a food processor fitted with the metal blade. Pulse on and off a few times to combine.

3 Add the chilled butter, tossing quickly with your fingers to coat with flour (this prevents the butter cubes from adhering together and helps them to combine more evenly with the flour). Pulse on and off about 15 times, until the mixture resembles small peas.

4 With the motor running, add the ice water all at once through the feed tube and process for about 10 seconds, stopping the machine before the dough becomes a solid mass.

5 Turn the dough out onto a sheet of aluminum foil, pressing any loose particles into the ball of dough. Form

6 On a lightly floured surface, roll out the dough to an 11-inch circle. Transfer to a baking sheet and trim the edges.

7 To make the filling, combine the cranberries, walnuts, superfine sugar, and brown sugar in a bowl. Toss to distribute the sugar evenly.

8 Spoon the cranberry mixture into the center of the dough round, leaving a 1 1/2-inch border all around the edge. Lift the dough border up over the filling, letting it drape gently over the fruit. Some of the filling will be exposed. Press down on the edges of the dough, snugly securing the sides and the bottom, being careful not to mash the fruit. Gently pinch together the pleats that have formed from the draping.

9 Bake the tart for 15 to 20 minutes, or until the crust is golden. Cool on a wire rack for about 10 minutes. Dust with confectioners' sugar and serve warm, with whipped cream, if desired.

▶ **The tart dough works best when made with very cold butter. This dough recipe makes enough for 2 nine-inch tart shells or 4 four-inch tartlet shells.**

◁ JOHANNE KILLEEN AND GEORGE GERMON: Cranberry-Walnut Tart

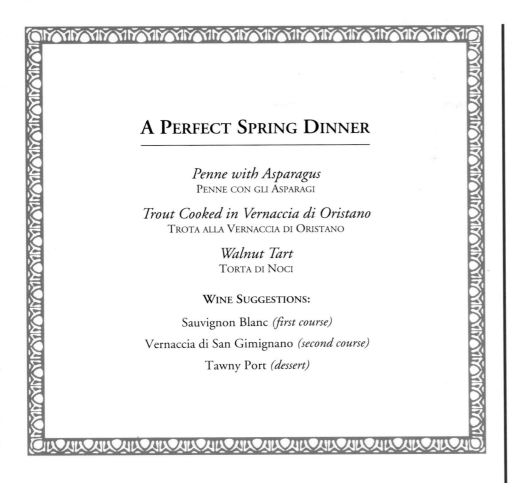

A PERFECT SPRING DINNER

Penne with Asparagus
PENNE CON GLI ASPARAGI

Trout Cooked in Vernaccia di Oristano
TROTA ALLA VERNACCIA DI ORISTANO

Walnut Tart
TORTA DI NOCI

WINE SUGGESTIONS:

Sauvignon Blanc *(first course)*

Vernaccia di San Gimignano *(second course)*

Tawny Port *(dessert)*

WHAT YOU CAN PREPARE AHEAD OF TIME

Up to 5 days ahead: Make the Walnut Tart. Cool, wrap tightly in aluminum foil, and refrigerate. Bring to room temperature before serving.

Early in the day: Prepare all the components for the Penne with Asparagus. Prepare all the components for the Trout Cooked in Vernaccia di Oristano.

Carlo Middione is the owner of Vivande restaurant and take-out food shop in San Francisco. His ancestors came from southern Italy, a region he clearly favors in his cooking—this sunny heritage virtually shines in all he teaches. Meals are always light and flavorful and, for the home cook, easy to prepare. I know that the recipes we have selected to represent Carlo's repertoire will become old standards in your kitchen.

◁ Springtime in Bellagio, Italy

Penne with Asparagus

Penne con gli Asparagi

Spring bursts forth with sweet asparagus peeking through this rich pasta dish. If you prefer, substitute another green vegetable.

1 pound thin asparagus stalks, trimmed and cut into 2-inch pieces
1/4 cup extra-virgin olive oil
2 cloves garlic, minced
1 1/2 pounds ripe Italian plum tomatoes, cored, peeled, seeded, and finely chopped
14 ounces dried penne
1 cup freshly grated Pecorino Romano cheese, plus extra for serving, if desired
2 large eggs, lightly beaten
Salt and freshly ground black pepper to taste

1 Assemble the *mise en place* trays for this recipe (see page 9).

2 Bring a large saucepan of water to a boil. When it boils, add salt and cook the asparagus for 4 minutes. Turn off the heat and, using a slotted spoon or tongs, transfer the asparagus to a bowl and cover to keep warm. Reserve the water for cooking the pasta.

3 In a large saucepan, heat the olive oil over medium heat. Add the garlic and cook for 2 to 3 minutes, until golden. Stir in the tomatoes and cook for about 10 minutes.

4 Meanwhile, return the asparagus water to a boil. Add the pasta and cook for 7 minutes, or until just barely *al dente*. Drain, leaving a little water clinging to the pasta.

5 Put the pasta in a large, heated casserole or a ceramic serving bowl set over a pan of simmering water. Stir in the asparagus and cheese. Add the beaten eggs and stir gently for 3 to 4 minutes, until the pasta is well coated and glossy. Stir in the tomato sauce and season to taste with salt and pepper. Serve immediately on warm dinner plates, with extra grated cheese passed at the table if desired.

▶ To heat the casserole, set it in a warm (250 degree F.) oven while you prepare the rest of the dish.

▶ The heat of the penne actually cooks the eggs. Adding the cheese before the eggs creates an insulation that keeps the eggs from getting too hot too quickly and curdling.

▷ CARLO MIDDIONE: **Penne with Asparagus**

Trout Cooked in
Vernaccia di Oristano

SERVES 6
PREPARATION TIME: ABOUT 30 MINUTES
COOKING TIME: ABOUT 30 MINUTES

Trota alla Vernaccia di Oristano

Vernaccia di Oristano wine from Sardegna is as different as night from day from the better-known Vernaccia di San Gimignano, a Tuscan wine. It is not yet readily available in American markets, and Carlo Middione suggests approximating the taste of Vernaccia di Oristano by mixing three parts California golden sherry with one part dry white vermouth. For that essential undertaste of bitterness so characteristic of the wine, Carlo adds a well-crushed kernel from the pit of a peach or apricot per quart of the wine mixture. This, he says, adds just enough of the amaro taste, which gives "ballast" to the flavor of the finished dish.

1/3 cup extra-virgin olive oil
2 cloves garlic, minced
1 large carrot, peeled and finely chopped
1 large yellow onion, finely chopped
2 ribs celery, finely chopped
1 large, ripe tomato, cored, peeled, seeded, and finely chopped
1 lemon, washed and thinly sliced
1/3 cup chopped fresh parsley
1/2 teaspoon ground oregano
Salt and freshly ground black pepper to taste
6 eight-ounce trout, cleaned
About 2 cups Vernaccia de Oristano, or a mixture of sherry and dry vermouth (see above)

1 Assemble the *mise en place* trays for this recipe (see page 9).

2 In a sauté pan large enough to hold all the trout, heat the olive oil. Add the garlic and sauté oven medium heat for 3 minutes, or until deep gold. Stir in the carrots, onions, celery, tomatoes, lemon, parsley, and oregano. Add salt and pepper to taste. Cook, stirring, for about 10 minutes, or until all the vegetables are lightly browned.

3 Reduce the heat and spread the vegetables evenly over the bottom of the pan. Arrange the trout snugly on top of the vegetables. Add enough wine to come halfway up the trout. Cover loosely with a lid or foil and cook for 5 minutes. Carefully turn the trout with a slotted spatula and cook for about 5 minutes more, or until cooked through. Remove the trout to a warm platter and cover with aluminum foil to keep warm.

4 Strain the vegetables and pan liquid through a fine sieve, pushing down on the solids to extract all the juices. Discard the solids. Pour the cooking liquid into a medium-sized saucepan and simmer over medium heat for about 10 minutes, or until reduced to 1 cup.

5 Place the trout on serving plates and spoon the sauce over the top. Serve immediately.

▶ Since this dish must be cooked at the last minute, organize your *mise en place* trays well to speed preparation.

▶ You may need to use 2 sauté pans, particularly if you decide to leave the heads on the trout for presentation purposes.

▶ California golden sherry is made by such wineries as Christian Brothers and Almaden. Good dry white vermouth is made by Cinzano and Martini and Rossi. Vermouth has a higher alcohol content than a dry white wine and, therefore, is more in keeping with the spirit of the Vernaccia di Oristano.

◁ CARLO MIDDIONE: Trout cooked in Vernaccia di Oristano

Walnut Tart

Torta di Noce

The key elements here are the walnuts and the *mosto cotto*, a jelly-like substance made from wine must. A good substitution for *mosto cotto* in this recipe is tart, lemony-tasting, red currant jelly.

PASTRY:

2 cups all-purpose unbleached flour, or more if necessary
1/3 cup granulated sugar
1/4 cup lard or solid vegetable shortening
1/4 cup unsalted butter
Grated zest of 1 lemon
1 large egg
3 to 4 large egg yolks

FILLING:

2 cups coarsely chopped walnuts
1/2 cup raisins
1/4 cup finely chopped candied orange peel
1 1/3 cups *mosto cotto* or 1 cup red currant jelly
1 large egg, beaten, for egg glaze

■ Special Equipment: Special equipment: 9-inch fluted tart pan with a removable bottom

1 Preheat the oven to 350 degrees F. Assemble the *mise en place* trays for this recipe (see page 9).

2 To make the pastry, combine the flour, sugar, lard, butter, and lemon zest in a food processor fitted with the metal blade. Pulse on and off 8 to 10 times, until the mixture resembles coarse crumbs. Add the egg and 3 egg yolks, and process until the dough just comes together. If the dough seems too wet, add additional flour, 1 teaspoon at a time. If the dough is too dry and won't hold together, add 1 more egg yolk.

3 Scrape the dough onto a lightly floured work surface and knead for 1 minute, or until quite soft. Form into a ball, wrap in plastic wrap, and refrigerate for 1 hour.

4 Meanwhile, make the filling. Stir together the walnuts, raisins, orange peel, and *mosto cotto* or jelly. Set aside.

5 Divide the dough in half. On a lightly floured surface, roll out half the dough to a 12-inch circle. Fit it into a 9-inch fluted tart pan with a removable bottom, leaving about a 1 1/2-inch overhang.

6 Spoon the filling into the tart pan, spreading it evenly.

7 Roll out the remaining piece of dough to a 12-inch circle. Lay the circle on top of the filling. Press the 2 layers of overhanging dough together and then roll up and over to make a raised edge, using your thumb and index finger to flute the edge. Make sure the edge is well sealed.

8 Using a pastry brush, coat the top of the tart with the egg glaze. Insert a small pastry tip into the center of the tart for a steam vent, or cut a cross-hatch in the center of the pastry. Then cut several 1/2-inch slashes in a decorative pattern over the surface to help steam escape. Set the tart on a baking sheet to catch any juices that escape during baking.

9 Bake for 55 to 60 minutes, or until nicely browned. Transfer to a wire rack to cool for 10 minutes. Remove the tart ring, cut the tart into wedges and serve warm. Or let cool before serving.

▶ **To facilitate removing the tart from the pan, place it, while still hot, on a bowl that is smaller than the tart pan, or on a large can. The ring will slip down and the tart will be supported by the metal bottom. If the ring does not slide down of its own accord, apply gentle pressure to the edges to loosen it.**

▶ **You may be able to buy *mosto cotto* in an Italian market or from a winery. Or, if you live near a winery, you may be able to buy wine must, which is juice freshly squeezed from grapes. If so, make *mosto cotto* by boiling the must in a heavy pan until it reduces to a thick, jelled consistency. Cool and use as you would any jelly.**

▷ CARLO MIDDIONE: Walnut Tart

A MEAL FROM MODENA

Parmesan Ice Cream
GELATO AL PARMIGIANO

Spinach Tart
ERBAZZONE

Fillet of Beef in the Modena Manner
FILETTO DI MANZO ALL'ACETO BALSAMICO TRADIZIONALE DI MODENA

Sour Cherry Tart
CROSTATA DI AMARENE

WINE SUGGESTIONS:

Champagne *(first course)*

Champagne *(second course)*

Chianti Classico *(third course)*

Ruby Port *(dessert)*

WHAT YOU CAN PREPARE AHEAD OF TIME

Up to 2 days ahead: Make the Parmesan Ice Cream.

Early in the day: Assemble the Spinach Tart. Cover and refrigerate until 1 hour before baking. Brush with the egg wash just before baking. Prepare the Fillet of Beef for roasting. Cover and refrigerate until 1 hour before roasting. Bake the Sour Cherry Tart. Warm just before serving, if desired.

M arta Pulini first taught at De Gustibus when she was the chef at Le Madri restaurant in New York City. Now executive chef at mad.61, the restaurant located in New York's famed Barney's uptown store on Madison Avenue, Marta has a most direct way of explaining her style of cooking. Not surprisingly, she favors the foods from the region around Modena, where she grew up, often giving favorite family recipes cosmopolitan flair. Exuding love for food, Marta reflects her long time passion for the kitchen. Attending her class, you feel as though you have been embraced by a storybook Italian mother. This menu is a taste of some of the dishes with which Marta Pulini grew up.

◁ MARTA PULINI: **Parmesan Ice Cream (recipe on page 78)**

Parmesan Ice Cream

Gelato al Parmigiano

This gelato is heavenly. The taste is so smooth and rich that nobody can guess exactly how it is made. And certainly your guests will never suspect how easy it has been to "wow" them! This is wonderful, too, as a cheese course or as an hors d'oeuvre at a cocktail party.

3 1/2 cups freshly grated Parmigiano-Reggiano cheese
2 cups plus 2 tablespoons heavy cream
1/8 teaspoon freshly ground white pepper
1 loaf Italian bread
3 firm pears, such as Bosc or Anjou
6 very small bunches of grapes, washed and dried
1 tablespoon balsamic vinegar, or to taste

1 In the top of a double boiler set over boiling water, combine the grated cheese, cream, and pepper. Cook, stirring continuously, for 5 minutes, or until the cheese is completely melted and the mixture is smooth. Remove from the heat and pour through a fine strainer into a shallow pan. Cool slightly and then cover and refrigerate for at least 12 hours.

2 Preheat the oven to 300 degrees F. Assemble the *mise en place* trays for the remaining ingredients (see page 9).

3 Slice the bread on the diagonal into at least 18 pieces about 1/4 inch thick. Place on a baking sheet on the bottom rack of the oven and bake, turning several times, for 25 to 35 minutes, or until dry and golden brown. Set aside.

4 To serve, peel the pears. Cut in half lengthwise and remove the core. Slice each pear half lengthwise into thin slices, and fan out one pear half on each chilled serving plate. Scoop a heaping spoonful of gelato at the base of the pear fan. Add a bunch of grapes and 3 slices of bread. Drizzle a few drops of balsamic vinegar over the gelato and serve immediately. Pass any remaining bread.

Spinach Tart

Erbazzone

This tart can be served warm or at room temperature, and as either an appetizer or a main course. What more could any home cook ask?

DOUGH:

2 ¾ cup plus 2 tablespoons unbleached, all-purpose flour

½ teaspoon salt, or to taste

1 cup (16 tablespoons) unsalted butter, cut into small pieces, chilled

4 to 6 tablespoons ice water

FILLING:

3 pounds fresh spinach, washed and tough stems removed

¼ pound pancetta, diced

1 clove garlic, minced

About 2 tablespoons olive oil, if necessary

1 bunch scallions, trimmed and sliced

1 bunch fresh flat-leaf parsley, stems discarded and leaves chopped

2 cups freshly grated Parmigiano-Reggiano cheese

Freshly ground black pepper to taste

2 large eggs

4 cups fresh bread crumbs

1 large egg yolk beaten with 1 tablespoon milk, for egg wash

■ Special Equipment: 12-inch fluted tart pan with removable bottom

1 Assemble the *mise en place* trays for this recipe (see page 9).

2 To make the dough, mound the flour and salt on a work surface and make a well in the center. Add the butter and, using your fingertips, rub into the flour until the mixture resembles small peas. Stir in the ice water a little at a time, until the dough just holds together. Form into a ball, wrap in plastic wrap and refrigerate for at least 30 minutes.

3 Preheat the oven to 350 degrees F. Generously butter a 12-inch fluted tart pan with a removable bottom.

4 To make the filling, blanch the spinach in a large pot of boiling water for 10 seconds. (Depending on the size of the

MARTA PULINI: **Spinach Tart**

pot, you may have to do this in two batches.) Drain well and refresh under cold running water. Drain again and let cool slightly. Squeeze out all the excess water from the spinach and chop it. Place it in a colander placed over a plate so that it can continue to drain, and set aside.

5 In a large sauté pan, cook the pancetta over medium heat for 4 to 5 minutes, to render the fat. Add the garlic and cook for 2 to 3 minutes, or just until the garlic starts to brown. Add 1 to 2 tablespoons of olive oil if the pan seems dry. Stir in the spinach and scallions and cook for 3

79

to 5 minutes, until the spinach has wilted. Transfer to a large bowl and stir in the parsley and cheese. Season to taste with pepper. Allow to cool for about 15 minutes.

6 Add the eggs and bread crumbs to the spinach mixture and stir to combine.

7 Divide the dough into 2 pieces, one slightly larger than the other. On a well-floured surface, roll out the larger piece to a 14-inch circle. Carefully fit into the prepared tart pan. Spoon the spinach filling into the tart shell, spreading it evenly and smoothing the top.

8 Roll out the remaining dough to a thin, 12-inch circle. Lay the circle on top of the filling and pull the overhanging dough up over it. Press the edges of dough together and pinch them to make a raised edge, using your thumb and index finger to flute the edge. Prick the top with a fork. Using a pastry brush, coat the top of the tart with the egg wash.

9 Bake the tart for 30 minutes, or until the top is golden. Remove from the oven and let rest for 5 minutes. Remove the tart ring, cut into wedges, and serve.

▶ If time is an issue, substitute 1¾ pounds (3 ten-ounce boxes) frozen chopped spinach. Thaw it and squeeze as much moisture as possible from it before proceeding with the recipe. (This eliminates at least 30 minutes of preparation time, as cleaning and stemming fresh spinach is tedious work.)

▶ The tart dough is fragile. Take care when working with it, but if it rips, simply smooth it together again. The dense filling does not require a flawless crust.

Fillet of Beef in the Modena Manner

Filetto di Manzo All'Aceto Balsamico Tradizionale di Modena

This is an easy-to-prepare dinner party main course. Use the absolute best Aceto Balsamico Tradizionale Di Modena (balsamic vinegar) to finish, for the authentic taste.

2 pounds beef tenderloin, trimmed of all fat
1 bunch fresh sage
1 bunch fresh thyme
4 sprigs fresh rosemary
2 cloves garlic, peeled
Salt and freshly ground black pepper to taste
2 tablespoons unsalted butter
2 tablespoons olive oil
3 tablespoons fine-quality balsamic vinegar

1 Preheat the oven to 400 degrees F. Assemble the *mise en place* trays for this recipe (see page 9).

2 Using a very sharp knife, butterfly the tenderloin by cutting it almost in half down its entire length. Open out and flatten slightly.

3 Chop all the herbs and the garlic very fine and mix together. Add salt and pepper to taste and chop again to mix. Sprinkle half the mixture over the cut side of the meat. Reshape the fillet and, using kitchen twine, tie in 6 or 8 places along the length. Rub the outside with the remaining herb mixture.

4 In a large roasting pan, melt the butter with the olive oil over medium-high heat. Add the meat and sear until well browned on all sides. Transfer to the oven and roast for 12 minutes. Turn the meat and cook for 12 minutes more for rare meat; for medium-rare meat, cook for 18 minutes on each side. Remove from the oven and allow to rest for a few minutes.

5 Slice the meat crosswise into ¼-inch slices, discarding the twine, and fan out on a warm serving platter. Drizzle with the balsamic vinegar and serve immediately.

MARTA PULINI: Fillet of Beef in the Modena Manner

Sour Cherry Tart

Crostata di Amarene

The sour cherry tart with its pretty latticed top is an appealing dessert to serve at the end of a special meal.

DOUGH:

1¾ cups plus 2 tablespoons all-purpose flour
½ cup plus 2 tablespoons granulated sugar
1½ teaspoons baking powder
Grated zest of 1 lemon
1 large egg plus 1 large egg yolk, lightly beaten
9 tablespoons unsalted butter, chilled

FILLING:

4 cups pitted fresh sour cherries
¾ cup granulated sugar
Grated zest of 1 orange
1 vanilla bean, split
1 tablespoon all-purpose flour
1 large egg yolk beaten with 1 tablespoon milk, for egg wash

■ Special Equipment: 9-inch fluted tart pan with a removable bottom

1 Assemble the *mise en place* trays for this recipe (see page 9).

2 To make the dough, combine the flour, sugar, baking powder, and lemon zest and mound on a clean work surface. Make a well in the center. Add the beaten egg and butter and, using your fingertips, rub into the flour until the dough just holds together. Form into a ball, wrap in plastic wrap, and refrigerate for at least 30 minutes.

3 Preheat the oven to 375 degrees F. Generously butter a 9-inch fluted tart pan with a removable bottom.

4 To make the filling, combine the cherries, sugar, orange zest, and vanilla bean in a medium-sized saucepan set over low heat. Cook over low heat, stirring frequently, for 35 to 50 minutes, until the mixture resembles chunky preserves (the time depends on the type of cherries). Remove from the heat and allow to cool for 15 minutes. Remove the vanilla bean.

5 Cut off about a quarter of the dough, rewrap the smaller piece, and refrigerate it. On a lightly floured surface, roll the larger piece of dough to a 12-inch circle. Fit it into the prepared tart pan. Trim the overhanging dough and combine trimmings with reserved dough.

6 Sprinkle the flour over the bottom of the tart shell. Spoon the cherry filling into the shell, smoothing the top.

7 Divide the reserved dough into 8 to 10 pieces and form into long strips by rolling them between the floured palms of your hands. Use the strips to make a widely spaced lattice top, pushing the ends of the ropes into the edges of the bottom shell. Trim off the excess dough.

8 Using a pastry brush, lightly coat the latticework and the edge of the tart with the egg wash. Bake for 30 to 35 minutes, until the crust is golden. Cool for 5 to 10 minutes on a wire rack. Then remove the tart ring, cut the tart into wedges, and serve warm.

▶ Sour cherries are in season in midsummer. If you cannot find frozen or dried cherries, use canned. For this recipe, you will need 2 16-ounce cans unsweetened sour cherries packed in water. Drain them well. (Do not use cherry pie filling or sweet cherries!) You can also substitute dried cherries by reconstituting them in warm water for about 30 minutes.

▷ MARTA PULINI: **Sour Cherry Tart**

CASUAL ITALIAN FARE

ANTIPASTI:

Broccoli Rabe, Garlic, and Pignoli Nuts
CIME DI RAPE AGLIO OLIO CON PIGNOLI

Roasted Carrots, Oregano, Rosemary, and Fontina Cheese
CAROTE ARROSTITE ALLA PIEMONTESE

Roasted Fennel, Thyme, and Parmigiano
FINOCCHIO ARROSTITO AL PARMIGIANO E TIMO

White Pizza with Arugula
PIZZA BIANCA CON RUCOLA

Walnut Biscotti
BISCOTTI ALLE NOCI

WINE SUGGESTIONS:

Champagne *(Antipasto course)*

Champagne *(second course)*

Vin Santo *(dessert)*

WHAT YOU CAN PREPARE AHEAD OF TIME

Up to 1 week ahead: Make the Walnut Biscotti. Store in an airtight container in a cool, dry place.

Early in the day: Prepare the antipasto. Cover and refrigerate. Bring to room temperature before serving. Make the dough for the White Pizza with Arugula. Wrap in plastic wrap and refrigerate. Bring to room temperature before baking. Prepare the arugula and garlic for the pizza topping.

Claudio Scadutto's De Gustibus class was pure joy! We had been dazzled by the tantalizing antipasto bar at his home base, Trattoria dell'Arte in New York City, and he brought a sampling of these inviting vegetable antipasto recipes with him to share with the students. Each one was more delicious than the one before, and, when served together, provided a feast of colors, shapes, and textures. Add Chef Scadutto's pizza for the perfect casual meal. To complete the De Gustibus experience, however, you need Claudio singing opera as he works. What an Italian event!

◁ CLAUDIO SCADUTTO: Walnut Biscotti (recipe on page 90)

Antipasto

SERVES 6
PREPARATION TIME (ALL 3 ANTIPASTI): ABOUT 40 MINUTES
COOKING TIME (ALL 3 ANTIPASTI): ABOUT 40 MINUTES

This selection is only the beginning. Use your imagination and let your creativity fly. An antipasto platter can be filled with any variety of cold meats, vegetables, and condiments.

The following recipes are designed to serve 6 people. If one recipe particularly appeals to you, the ingredients can easily be doubled to increase your antipasto bounty.

BROCCOLI RABE, GARLIC, AND PIGNOLI NUTS
Cime di Rape Aglio Olio con Pignoli

2 pounds broccoli rabe (about 2 bunches)
4 cloves garlic, minced
1/4 cup toasted pignoli nuts (pine nuts; see page 12)
1/4 cup extra-virgin olive oil
Salt to taste

1 Assemble the *mise en place* trays for this recipe (see page 9).

2 Soak the broccoli rabe in cold water to cover for about 15 minutes. Drain well. Trim off any large leaves and the tough stem ends. Using a small sharp knife, cut slashes into the stalks. Using the kitchen twine, tie the broccoli rabe into bunches.

3 In a large deep saucepan of boiling, salted water, cook the broccoli rabe, standing it upright so that the heads are covered by about 1 inch of water for 4 to 5 minutes, until just tender and bright green. Drain well and remove the twine.

4 Arrange the broccoli rabe on a serving platter or in a shallow bowl. Gently toss with the garlic, nuts, olive oil, and salt to taste. Serve at room temperature.

▶ **This is also delicious served over pasta for a quick dinner.**

◁ CLAUDIO SCADUTTO: Antipasto: Broccoli Rabe, Garlic, and Pignoli Nuts; Roasted Carrots, Oregano, Rosemary, and Fontina Cheese; Roasted Fennel, Thyme, and Parmigiano

ROASTED CARROTS, OREGANO, ROSEMARY, AND FONTINA CHEESE
Carote Arrostite alla Piemontese

8 carrots, peeled and sliced diagonally into 1/2-inch thick slices
3 tablespoons extra-virgin olive oil
Salt and freshly ground black pepper to taste
2 teaspoons minced fresh oregano
2 teaspoons minced fresh rosemary
1/2 cup freshly shredded Fontina cheese

1 Preheat the oven to 350 degrees F. Assemble the *mise en place* trays for this recipe (see page 9).

2 In a shallow baking dish, combine the carrots with the olive oil and salt and pepper to taste, and toss lightly to coat. Roast for 35 minutes, or until just slightly crisp.

3 Transfer the carrots to a serving platter. Sprinkle with the minced herbs and cheese. Serve at room temperature.

ROASTED FENNEL, THYME, AND PARMIGIANO
Finocchio Arrostito al Parmigiano e Timo

3 small fennel bulbs, washed, trimmed, cored, and quartered lengthwise
1/4 cup extra-virgin olive oil
Salt and freshly ground black pepper to taste
2 teaspoons minced fresh thyme
1 three-ounce piece Parmigiano-Reggiano cheese

1 Preheat the oven to 350 degrees F. Assemble the *mise en place* trays for this recipe (see page 9).

2 In a shallow baking dish, combine the fennel with the olive oil and salt and pepper to taste, and toss lightly to coat. Roast for 30 to 35 minutes, or until light golden brown.

3 Transfer the fennel to a serving platter. Sprinkle with the thyme. Using a vegetable peeler or cheese slicer, shave the Parmigiano over the top. Serve at room temperature.

White Pizza with Arugula

SERVES 6
PREPARATION TIME: ABOUT 30 MINUTES
COOKING TIME (FOR ALL 6 PIZZAS AT 15 MINUTES PER
INDIVIDUAL PIZZA): 1 HOUR AND 30 MINUTES
RESTING TIME (DOUGH ONLY): ABOUT 2 HOURS

Pizza Bianca con Rucola

These delightfully crisp pizzas bear no resemblance to the soggy, fast-food variety. They are wonderfully fresh-tasting, with no tomato sauce or cheese. These little pizzas are best eaten directly from the oven. Serving them this way turns your party into an informal affair, as you continue to cook pizzas while others are being happily devoured.

PIZZA DOUGH:

3 cups water
1/4 cup sugar
One 1/4-ounce package active dry yeast
1/4 cup vegetable oil
1 tablespoon salt
1 1/2 cups plus 3 tablespoons bread flour
1 1/2 cups plus 3 tablespoons semolina flour

TOPPING:

3 cups packed finely shredded arugula
1/4 cup finely chopped garlic
3/4 to 1 cup extra-virgin olive oil

■ Special Equipment: Pizza stone.

1 Assemble the *mise en place* trays for this recipe (see page 9).

2 In a large, warm bowl, combine the water, sugar, and yeast. Stir to dissolve. Let rest for 15 minutes.

3 Stir the vegetable oil and salt into the yeast mixture. Add both the flours and mix with a wooden spoon or your hands to combine. Put the dough in a bowl, cover with a kitchen towel, and let stand for 20 minutes in a warm, draft-free place.

4 Turn the dough a few times in the bowl. Let stand 20 minutes longer.

5 Again, turn the dough and let stand 20 minutes.

6 Turn the dough out onto a lightly floured surface and knead dough for about 3 minutes, until smooth and elastic. Divide into 6 pieces and shape into balls. Leaving the balls on the floured surface, cover them with kitchen towels, and let rest for about 1 hour.

7 Put a pizza stone on the center rack of the oven and preheat the oven to 450 degrees F.

8 Flatten each piece of dough into a round, pushing it into a 6-inch circle with your fingertips. Place 1 pizza on the hot pizza stone and bake for about 15 minutes, or until golden. Remove from the oven and sprinkle with 1/2 cup of the arugula and 2 teaspoons of the garlic. Drizzle with olive oil and serve. Continue baking the remaining pizzas, serving each one as soon as it is assembled.

▶ **If you have 2 pizza stones, raise the oven temperature to 500 degrees F. and bake 2 pizzas at a time. If you don't have a pizza stone, you can bake the pizzas on a preheated heavy baking sheet, but the crusts will not be as crispy. Pizza stones are sold in kitchenware shops. You can also use unglazed ceramic tiles, found in kitchenware shops, instead of a pizza stone.**

▶ **You can make 2 large pizzas with the dough and the same amount of topping and serve them cut into wedges.**

◁ CLAUDIO SCADUTTO: White Pizza with Arugula

Walnut Biscotti

Biscotti alle Noci

Crisp biscotti are perfect for dunking in a cup of strong, rich espresso. Great keepers, they are a boon to have on hand for unexpected guests.

3 3/4 cups all-purpose flour
2 tablespoons baking powder
5 large eggs
1 1/2 cups sugar
1 vanilla bean or 1 teaspoon pure vanilla extract
1 1/2 cups chopped walnuts
1 1/2 cups vegetable oil

1 Preheat the oven to 350 degrees F. Assemble the *mise en place* trays for this recipe (see page 9). Line 2 baking sheets with parchment paper.

2 In a medium-sized bowl, whisk together the flour and baking powder. Set aside.

3 In a large bowl, using an electric mixer set on medium-high speed, beat the eggs and sugar together until light and creamy. Split the vanilla bean, if using, in half and scrape the seeds into the batter. Or add the vanilla extract, if using, and stir to combine. Add the walnuts and stir just to combine.

4 Stir the flour mixture into the batter, alternating it with the oil and mixing gently until incorporated.

5 Scrape about a quarter of the dough into a pastry bag fitted with a #2 plain tip, and pipe long cylinders of dough about 1 inch thick and about the width of the baking sheet onto the prepared sheets, leaving about 2 inches between each one. Refill the pastry bag and repeat with the remaining dough. Bake for 15 minutes, or until golden brown. Remove the baking sheets and leave the oven on.

6 Let the biscotti rest for about 5 minutes. Cut each cylinder on the diagonal into cookies about 3 inches long. The cookies are about 1/4 inch thick. Lay the cookies on the baking sheets and bake for 2 to 3 minutes longer. Transfer to wire racks to cool completely.

Glossary

Amaretti: Very light, crisp macaroon-type Italian cookies made with either apricot kernel paste or bitter almond paste.

Amaretto: Almond-flavored liqueur usually made from apricot kernels. Originally, Amaretto di Saronno was imported from Italy, but now it is distilled in the United States.

Antipasto: An assortment of Italian hors d'oeuvres, served (literally) "before the pasta."

Al dente: Italian term meaning, literally, "to the tooth." Most often used to describe pasta that has been cooked until it is just tender but still offers some resistance when chewed. Can also be used to describe the degree to which certain vegetables should be cooked.

Arborio rice: Medium-grain, plump, high-starch rice used in Italian cooking, most often to make the traditional risotto. The best is imported from Italy.

Arugula: An astringent, fragrant salad green with a sharp, peppery flavor. Also known as rocket and rucola. Highly perishable.

Balsamella: Italian for the basic French béchamel sauce made by stirring hot milk into a flour-butter roux. Also known as white or cream sauce.

Balsamic vinegar: Italian specialty vinegar that has been produced in Modena for centuries. It is made from the boiled-down must of white grapes. True balsamic vinegar is aged for decades in a succession of different types of wood barrels.

Bel Paese: Mild, buttery, semisoft Italian cow's milk cheese produced outside Milan. Literally translated, the name means "beautiful country."

Biscotti: Crisp, twice-baked, not-too-sweet Italian cookie traditionally dipped into strong coffee or dessert wine before being eaten.

Blanch: To plunge food briefly into boiling water to set color, texture, or both, or to help loosen the skin. Usually, the food is immediately placed in cold or ice water to stop the cooking process.

Bosc pear: A slender, firm-fleshed winter pear with blotchy, yellow-brown skin.

Broccoli rabe: A pungent, firm-stalked, leafy green with broccoli-like flowers, traditionally used in Italian cooking. Also known as broccoli raab or rape.

Cappuccino: Italian coffee made by topping espresso with hot, frothy, steamed milk. Ground cinnamon or cocoa may be sprinkled on top.

Caramel: The result of melting sugar to a thick, clear, golden-to-light-brown liquid. Depending on what is added to the sugar, caramel can become a sauce, a candy, or a flavoring.

Espresso: Strong Italian coffee, usually made by machine. Steam is forced through very finely ground aromatic coffee beans. Espresso can also be made on the stove top with boiling water.

Flute: To make a decorative edge on a pie by pressing the dough together between your thumb and index finger.

Fontina: Semisoft, nutty-tasting Italian cow's milk cheese with 45 percent butterfat. The best Fontina is Fontina Val d'Aosta, named for the Alpine region in which it originated.

Frittata: Italian omelet in which the flavoring ingredients are mixed into the eggs before they are cooked over low heat.

Gelato: Italian for ice cream or other frozen dishes with the texture of ice cream. Italian gelato is usually denser and less sweet and contains less fat than its American counterpart.

Gnocchi: Light, airy Italian dumplings made from potatoes, farina, or flour and occasionally flavored with cheese, eggs, or spinach. The literal translation is "little lumps."

Gorgonzola: Rich, creamy, blue-veined Italian cow's milk cheese with a strong, musty flavor. Best used as soon as it has been cut from a wheel, since it quickly loses moisture. Named for the town where it was first produced.

Julienne: Refers to foods, particularly vegetables, that have been cut into uniform thin strips, usually about the size of a matchstick. The vegetable to be julienned is first cut into slices of uniform thickness and then the slices are stacked and cut into even strips. Classically, these strips are one inch long by one quarter inch thick. Usually used as a decorative garnish.

Juniper berries: The berries from the juniper bush, these have a rather sweet, piney flavor. Usually sold dried, they are generally used to season sauces or vegetables. Juniper berries are also the benchmark flavor of gin. It is said that the world's best juniper berries come from the southern slopes of the Italian Alps.

Marsala: A sweet dessert wine.

Mascarpone: Sweet, soft, creamy cow's milk Italian cheese not unlike a very thick, slightly acidic whipped cream.

Mortadella: Italian smoked sausage made from ground pork and beef with added cubes of fat and aromatic seasonings.

Must: Freshly pressed grape juice.

Pancetta: Salt-cured, unsmoked, flavorful Italian bacon, frequently used to season soups, stews, and sauces.

Parma ham: see Prosciutto.

Parmigiano-Reggiano: Grainy, hard, dry, pale amber Italian part-skimmed cow's milk cheese with a sharp-sweet taste. Parmigiano-Reggiano is the most eminent of all Parmesan cheeses; its name is always stamped on the rind of cheeses produced in the areas surrounding the Parma and Reggio Emilia regions.

Pecorino Romano: Grainy, hard, dry, aged Italian sheep's milk cheese ranging in color from white to soft yellow, with a very pungent flavor. The best known of the pecorino (sheep) cheeses, it is generally grated for use in cooking and can be substituted for grated Parmesan cheese in many recipes; however, less is called for since it has a sharper taste.

Pignoli or pine nuts: Small, oval, fatty nuts from the cones of several varieties of pine trees.

Porcini mushrooms: Meaty wild mushroom of the *Boletus edulis* species, ranging in size from less than an ounce to more than a pound. Also known as cèpes, porcini are often sold dried.

Prosciutto: Italian salt-cured and air-dried ham that has been slow-aged for a dense texture and delicate, sweet flavor. Italy's parma ham is the traditional prosciutto.

Ricotta: Fresh, creamy Italian cheese made from the whey left from various cheeses. It is pale white, granular, and almost sweet-tasting.

Risotto: A rich, creamy Italian rice dish created by gradually stirring hot liquid into short-grained rice (such as Arborio) that has been sautéed in oil and aromatics.

Roux: A cooked mixture of flour and fat that is blended into liquids to thicken them.

Semolina flour: Coarsely ground durum wheat flour, traditionally used to make pasta.

Tirami-sù: Translated literally, this means "pick me up." It is a rich, traditional dessert made from mascarpone cheese and ladyfingers.

Vin santo: Amber-colored, intensely flavored Italian wine used as an apéritif or to accompany desserts. Produced in small quantities in the Chianti vineyards.

CONVERSION CHART

WEIGHTS AND MEASURES

1 teaspoon = 5 milliliters
1 tablespoon = 3 teaspoons = 15 milliliters
1/8 cup = 2 tablespoons = 1 fluid ounce = 30 milliliters
1/4 cup = 4 tablespoons = 2 fluid ounces = 59 milliliters
1/2 cup = 8 tablespoons = 4 fluid ounces = 118 milliliters
1 cup = 16 tablespoons = 8 fluid ounces = 237 milliliters
1 pint = 2 cups = 16 fluid ounces = 473 milliliters
1 quart = 4 cups = 32 fluid ounces = 946 milliliters (.946 liter)
1 gallon = 4 quarts = 16 cups = 128 fluid ounces = 3.78 liters

1 ounce = 28 grams
1/4 pound = 4 ounces = 114 grams
1 pound = 16 ounces = 454 grams
2.2 pounds = 1,000 grams = 1 kilogram

Index